KT-464-615

Wylie

Also by

One Dog at a Time: Saving the Strays of Helmand

No Place Like Home: A New Beginning with the Dogs of Afghanistan

Wylie

The brave street dog
who never gave up

PEN FARTHING

HODDER &
STOUGHTON

First published in Great Britain in 2014
by Hodder & Stoughton
An Hachette UK company

1

Copyright © Paul Farthing 2014

The right of Paul Farthing to be identified as the Author
of the Work has been asserted by him in accordance with
the Copyright, Designs and Patents Act 1988.

A CIP catalogue record for this title is available from the British Library

Hardback ISBN 978 1 444 79958 3
Trade Paperback ISBN 978 1 444 79959 0
Ebook ISBN 978 1 444 79957 6

Typeset in Cochin by Hewer Text UK Ltd, Edinburgh
Printed and bound by Clays Ltd, St Ives plc

Hodder & Stoughton policy is to use papers that are natural, renewable
and recyclable products and made from wood grown in sustainable
forests. The logging and manufacturing processes are expected to
conform to the environmental regulations of the country of origin.

Hodder & Stoughton Ltd
338 Euston Road
London NW1 3BH

www.hodder.co.uk

For Nowzad – the dog that changed my life
and was the cause of animal welfare in Afghanistan.
Bark all you want now. . .

Contents

A note from the Author

When I was invited to write my third book I jumped at the opportunity. And then I realised how different it would be from my first two books; this was not my story. It is the story of Wylie and his interaction with so many people who came into his life bringing good and bad along the way.

My starting point for what we did know about Wylie was when he arrived a bloodied mess at Kandahar airfield. We can never really know what happened to Wylie during his early years, unless we learn to talk dog I suppose, but this book is my take on Wylie's story.

Thanks to emails and face-to-face discussions with the various people who were involved I have pieced together most of his amazing story, interpreting all the correspondence and drawing it together so as to make a readable 'tail'.

With the unknown periods of Wylie's life during the early chapters I have had to use a small amount of poetic license and *improvise*, just as all Royal Marines both serving and retired are taught to improvise, adapt and overcome when the facts for battle are not present. And writing this book was a battle at times, the incredibly short time frame to hand in the manuscript that I was given was almost a show stopper on numerous occasions!

Each of the early chapters is based on true events, albeit to another person or dog in Afghanistan at some point.

For example; it is actually me who was the troop sergeant finding himself on an isolated track with a group of approaching elder Afghans. I had to explain how Aseel first met Danielle. Sitting in our staff room at the Nowzad clinic one day drinking tea with Aseel during the research for this book, I had listened intently as he explained how he had come across the old man looking for Kandahar airfield to find his injured son.

I could not believe it.

My first day on the ground in the village of Nowzad, in October 2006, saw me having a meeting with a different old man but sadly his mission had been the same; find a son injured during a Taliban attack who had been taken to Kandahar by the Americans. The man with the wheelbarrow was there too.

And Danielle does exist but I decided to change her name as I am unsure as to whether she would want her real name used. She did not contribute to the writing of this book or endorse it, any views or actions attributed to her do not necessarily represent her views or actions. Everything you read about the amazing things Danielle did to take care of her little animal welfare patch of Afghanistan is my interpretation of actual events – along with the training she was delivering to the ANP – as I understand it.

Again I have had to use poetic license for the voice I have given Danielle and depiction of her in this book but I hope I have done my best to give her full credit for the amazing things she achieved while serving in a war zone. All of us still think of Danielle as a true legend of animal rescue.

A NOTE FROM THE AUTHOR

From our experiences of running the only animal welfare shelter in Afghanistan both myself and Louise have pretty much seen all manner of things. The episode where Wylie loses his ears is sadly very much how it happens and both of us were overwhelmed when an elderly Afghan lady actually did bring in three young dogs that she had been feeding and caring for to the Nowzad shelter as she feared for their safety. Now and again there is a ray of hope for animal welfare in Afghanistan.

I'd like to say a really big thank you to those who gave up time to make sure I had all their facts and figures correct and for filling in the blanks especially; Aseel your positive outlook on the future of Afghanistan is an inspiration, Louise for dedicating her life to the animals of Afghanistan, Marnie and the whole team at PARSA (ukparsa.com, now a registered UK charity) for giving us the start we needed and the ongoing support, Melissa for her hard work and dedication at Nowzad HQ – the CiC appreciates it! To Tony and Sandi for being so strong and your determination with 353.org.uk (raising money for military charities) and of course Sarah for adopting Wylie. Sarah's interviews were conducted by recording voice notes on her phone. Sarah, your voice notes were just too funny!

And then there is Wylie. The little fluff ball is proof of the forgiving nature of dogs and I guess why we love them so much. Thanks Wylie for surviving and never giving up on people. As an ambassador for his fellow four legged companions left behind in Afghanistan he has done them proud.

Thank you so much to all at Hodder & Stoughton for publishing Wylie's amazing story; Elizabeth Caraffi, Kerry Hood, Ellie Cheele and Bea Long and of course a special thanks to Briony Gowlett for me giving me the opportunity to write once more and then for putting up with my delaying tactics in handing over the manuscript, and the last minute changes that were needed – thank you! I would also like to thank my copy editor, Belinda Jones for her very wise words!

To all of the Nowzad family of supporters and to those reading one of my books for the first time, thank you so much. Sadly we can't save all the animals that are in need but if we all do our bit then we can make a difference, even if it is just one dog at a time.

To Minnie and Orla; my two beautiful nieces – looking forward to coaching you both to Gold at the World Climbing Championships whilst you wear the red of Manchester!

To Nowzad, Tali, Patchdog and Maxchat; thank you for being consistently nightmares to look after!

And finally to my gorgeous and *intelligent* Hannah. #theone TMIT xxx

Pen F, September 2014
Follow me on twitter: @PenFarthing

Introduction

Wylie stole my heart the moment I watched a clip of him on Nowzad's Facebook page. Just scrolling down on my phone led to me crying and needing to share his plight with my friends.

Reading about the abuse he'd endured at the hands of man upset me enough, and that was before I'd even pressed play. Pictures of him out in Afghanistan mingling with the soldiers faded to pictures of his injuries and then to a short video clip of him lying on his back between someone's legs whilst they attended to a wound. He lay still letting them stitch him up, no struggle or yelp, just the occasional leg twitch as the pain took over. I'm sure he knew they were helping him, he trusted those that came to his aid. What a brave little dog I thought. Poor chap, how could anyone do that? From that moment Wylie was special to me.

When I got the opportunity to meet him, to apologise to him for what people had done, I jumped at the chance. I felt very lucky to be in the same kennel as him, amazed he was so jolly and affectionate. That was it; I had to see him again. He was a 45 minute drive away but I didn't care. When I

1

arrived Wylie would look forward to his walks down to the stream with his buddy AJ. He was always so pleased to see me. Saying goodbye for the last time was awful but he was off to his new life. When I got the call to say he couldn't go and would I foster him of course I said yes. To take him out of his kennel for the last time and put him in my car was a great feeling.

He settled in amazingly well for a dog who'd probably never been in a house before. He got on with my other dogs Ben and Milo straight away and from the first night they all slept together downstairs without a problem. Yes we've had some hiccups along the way with separation anxiety and food issues but he's *never* shown any aggression to people. After all he's been through he still loves everyone he meets, especially men which I find amazing since it would've most likely been men that abused him. He's not fazed by anything, he takes everything in his stride. Unlike so many of the Nowzad rescues who are terrified of fireworks, associating the bangs with the guns and bombs of their previous life, Wylie seems as if he couldn't care less.

Wylie's laid back nature and amazing story led me to enter him into the rescue classes at Scruffts and Buckham Fair. To tell people about him and raise awareness for Nowzad was my main aim. To be able to tell his story to a captive audience of hundreds was great. There were gasps from the crowds and cheers when he won and everyone wanted to meet the brave little guy. I duly handed out Nowzad leaflets to anyone who showed an interest and people would occasionally give me money for Nowzad as they were so moved.

Winning Scruffts with him was fantastic, what an experience! Although I knew it would be televised I hadn't really thought about us going on TV and doing interviews. It was nerve wracking and exciting all at the same time. But Wylie wasn't fazed by the cameras, lights and people rushing about in the studios. Throughout it all I was more nervous than him. He would just lay down and doze off whilst my heart was racing! People have commented that after all he's been through did he really need to go to big dog shows and on TV? I would never have done it if I thought he couldn't handle it. He breezes through whatever situation I put him in. You only have to see him trotting along a platform, tail wagging, after getting off a tube train to see he's ok. Or how he wants to see everyone and soak up the attention. He trusts me and I would never let him have reason to doubt me.

Wylie is an amazing dog. He's made me more determined than ever to help Nowzad. His funny little ways and the utter chaos he's brought to my life is something I'd never want to change. Sometimes I still think it's odd that the furry ball laying on the sofa or in front of the fire is the dog I saw on that clip. A dog from Afghanistan is in my house, a dog who was so let down by mankind is now part of a home. I'm so proud of him for everything, for being so trusting and kind. I still get upset thinking about his past and even writing this has been emotional, but for Wylie the future is bright and happy. Wylie I love you xx

Sarah Singleton,
September 2014

chapter 1

Wrong Place, Wrong Time

The sun had yet to have any warming influence on the frigid, early morning air that hugged the rocky desert floor. The landscape, bearing more resemblance to a barren, airless moonscape than anywhere remotely habitable, was not a place that seemed to encourage life to flourish.

But, against all the odds, it did.

The brindle-coloured pup, with all four paws white, as if he was wearing ankle socks, looked completely out of place as he wandered across the cold, arid ground, searching for any morsel of food, no matter how minuscule. The puppy was hungry. Very hungry.

Curled up alone last night, the puppy had been really cold – the thermometers in the nearby airfield had clocked the mercury well below minus fifteen, the military helicopters undergoing a meticulous de-icing routine before authority was given for them to lift off into the night sky. The puppy's short brown fur gave him some slender but brief-lived protection from the bitter cold. It would be several weeks until his coat was thick enough to keep him warm. Until then, he would shiver himself awake every few minutes.

And he missed his mum. A lot. The four-socked puppy had loved the affection his mum had shown him – only a young, feral dog herself, she had continuously licked at the clumps of dirt matted into his tiny body, a never-ending labour of love to remove them. Weak and undernourished, he had struggled to stay upright as she roughly prodded and poked his ears with her tongue, never satisfied he was clean enough. Socks hadn't minded, though: he would just snuggle closer into her, not wanting the moment to end. But, of course, it would always have to come to an end as she had her other pups to take care of, gently nudging him aside so she could tend to them as well.

But she was not there to do that now.

His uniquely white-socked paws and white patch on his chest were now stained a dirty mud colour, the former brilliance of his flashy white patch whilst under the care of his mum long gone.

Skinny little Socks had no idea where his mum was. He had not seen her for days. Only the memory of squabbling for space to suckle against her scruffy, unkempt body along with his noisily chirping brothers and sisters in the small dirt hollow they called home remained, their combined warmth fighting off the effects of the southern Afghan winter as it bit hard during the early weeks of January.

But then, one day, having departed as she normally did after the early morning feed – no doubt looking for food of her own so she could continue to nourish her demanding litter – she had just not come back.

Huddled together for warmth, his brothers and sisters had waited patiently for her to return but then, one by one, as hunger started to gnaw in the pit of their tiny stomachs, they too had left in search of food. And now only he remained behind. Socks. Scared, alone and confused.

Eventually, hunger drove him too from the safety of their rocky hollow. With no sign or smell of his siblings, he now wandered aimlessly around the barren, rubbish-strewn expanse of desert, which felt so big and alien to him.

As he picked his way across the empty ground, sniffing at bits of unrecognisable plastic and dross left by people with nowhere else to discard it, he noticed a glass bottle, its neck broken and gleaming in the early morning sunlight, leaning upright against a shattered rock. The long-since empty bottle didn't really look out of place in the desert graveyard of rubbish, but it fascinated the curious pup. A yellow piece of paper inside smelt sweet as he sniffed deeply, running his moist nose along the smooth glass. His bushy, pipe-cleaner-like tail wagged crazily as he investigated the new smell as, just for a moment, he was diverted from his never-ending quest for food.

The early morning breeze sought out the exposed openings in the Taliban fighter's clothing. His body already numb from the hours spent lying prone in the darkness, his flimsy, cotton *salwar kameez*, discoloured and faded from constant wearing, was scant protection from the Afghan winter. But he hardly noticed the chill and tried to dismiss the annoyance as he would a bothersome fly that plagued every waking hour of the summer months in this part of the world.

The fully stocked ammunition pouches on the old Soviet combat webbing waistcoat he wore doing did nothing to bring comfort to the position he was lying in, either. But the discomfort was bearable and simply a means to an end.

The Taliban *mujahideen* looked once again along the rusting barrel of his AK-47 assault rifle, through the single iron
sight at the end of the rifle's muzzle, chipped and pitted
from the years of resting his trusted weapon with the muzzle
to the ground – a habit that would have earned him the
wrath of any British weapons instructor had he joined the
pro-Government forces. He stared across the featureless
terrain that lay in his field of fire, watching over what was,
at the moment, an empty stretch of road below his firing
position.

The road had been ploughed from the American airbase
in Kandahar through a harsh, rugged landscape of broken
rock and arid land unsuitable for farming, as it hugged the
hillside down to his right and dipped out of view. The road
builders had been forced into a turn by a sheer, jutting ridge
of rock – a bend that caused any vehicle to slow as the road
crested a small hill and the drivers turned onto the flat
stretch of road that the Taliban fighter was currently watching with interest. This was Highway 1, linking Kandahar to
Kabul and beyond, to lands that the *mujahideen* fighter had
no interest in, nor would ever see.

Lying on the cold desert ground, amongst the discarded
plastic bottles and other items that were littered around, he
was just hidden from view, the bulk of his slim body out of
sight in a steep-sided *wadi* that had been carved from the
hardened earth by the flash-flooding that occurred as the
mountain snow melted and the rain arrived.

If all went well today then he had seen his last snow melt,
a fact that did not bother him.

He had been lying as still as he possibly could for three
hours, now and again lifting his head slightly to scan further
afield, the weak winter sun just now rising above the jagged

backdrop of the eastern mountains, orange and yellow hues fanning out to claim the brightening blue sky.

It was almost time. He was surprised that he did not feel more nervous. Just a casual acceptance of what was to come. His path to martyrdom was preordained, just like his Taliban brothers next to him. Together they had completed the many arduous months of brutal training required by their brigade *mullah*, learning fighting tactics in the harsh, wild tribal lands between Afghanistan and Pakistan.

He could barely feel his hands and feet as the cold had crept into his limbs, but the anticipation of his future actions had kept the fire in his belly alive. He knew two of his *mujahideen* brothers were only yards away to his right, scanning the area of road adjacent to him.

Even though he had not heard a sound from them in the last three hours, he did not need to risk moving his head to verify they were still there. Just like him, they were *mujahideen* fighters, sworn to fight *jihad* against the foreign invaders. He knew they would be as awake and alert as he was.

Once more he scanned for signs of the cowardly westerners, slowly putting out his right hand, ignoring the cold-induced stiffness to wrap his fingers around the long wooden barrel of the rocket-propelled-grenade launcher positioned ready by his side. He felt a resurgence of confidence.

'*Insha'Allah*,' he thought to himself. *If God wills it*. He let the plan of attack play out in his head for the last time. The version he ran through always ended the same way: he was welcomed into the arms of God. His sacrifice pleasing the one true God. His *mullah* had promised them all that their attack would send fear into the heart of the western soldiers, reminding them that Afghanistan was not so easily taken – a lesson the Soviets had learnt the hard way.

He was brought back to the bitter, real world of his surroundings by the throaty growl of a heavy vehicle's engine as it ground through the gears, accelerating out of the turn on the road and into his line of view.

His body shook off the chill as all his senses came online at once.

It was a Warthog armoured vehicle, its desert-coloured, steel-plated square sides giving it the appearance of a heavy box on tracks. It was the British Army's hastily adapted but improved version of the Bronco all-terrain vehicle, which was employed by the Singaporean Armed Forces. Much to the relief of the troops who had to travel in them, Procurement had realised that the standard version had never endured combat operations and change had been needed for tactical suitability in the harsh reality of Afghanistan. This included specially designed anti-RPG cages that cocooned the hull of all Warthogs operating in Afghanistan.

To the Taliban fighter, it was just a moving target.

The lead Warthog of the small convoy rumbled into the Taliban fighter's arc of fire as it came out of the right-hand turn in the road. The 350-brake horse-power engine churned out a pungent cloud of diesel fumes as the driver increased his speed into the straight.

Scanning the road, the fighter checked for the marker – a clear broken bottle, with a yellow piece of paper purposefully pushed inside – which was to anybody else just another piece of discarded trash amongst the million other pieces. He had placed the marker days before when, along with his two *mujahideen* brothers, disguised as goat herders, they had recce'd the firing positions they now occupied. The morning sun caught the remaining section of the neck of the bottle and it glinted back at him. Just as he had planned.

A slight movement. He quickly glanced to the left of the bottle, amongst the broken rocks pushed to the side of the road. He was distracted for a second as his brain puzzled as to what it was.

A shabby-looking, grey-coloured puppy with a white chest and four white paws, no more than two months old he guessed, was slowly sniffing the ground as it stumbled along towards the bottle.

The Taliban fighter gave it no more thought. Dogs were dirty, and hundreds of the disgusting creatures roamed these lands. They were of no interest to him. Especially now.

The lead vehicle was less than 100 yards away from his marker and the scavenging puppy. Two more vehicles had now come into view, all increasing speed to maintain their distance to the vehicle in front as they bore onto the straight.

Three seconds.

Two seconds.

One second.

He counted down in Pashto silently in his head. Then, without hesitation, he scooped up the rocket-propelled-grenade launcher as he forced his stiff body into the braced, crouching position he had been taught, over and over again.

The wooden shoulder mount fitted glove-like into his right shoulder as he brought the weapon to bear. The safety catch was already off.

He took one deep breath and held it as he lined up the simple sighting system against the square silhouette of the front Warthog as it sped along the road, steadily twisting his upper body to the left as he matched the vehicle's speed with the end of the RPG warhead. His right index finger squeezed the cold, metallic trigger as the unsuspecting armoured vehicle drew level with the marker.

The noise was deafening as the rocket ignited with a thunderous roar and sped lethally towards the lead vehicle as the stabilising fins deployed, the warhead's path marked by a vapour trail.

He threw the now useless launcher to the ground as two similar vapour trails arced over the rubbish-strewn wasteland towards the second and third vehicles. He turned his head to smile as his brothers dropped their own used launchers to the ground.

'*Allah Akbar!*' he shouted as he charged out of his hiding place, his eyes focused on the lead vehicle.

It had skidded to a halt across the now pitted asphalt, black smoke billowing from the point of impact where the explosive warhead had struck the anti-RPG cage.

With adrenalin surging through his veins, he stormed across the open ground, his faith now guiding him as, with his AK-47 pulled tightly into his shoulder, pumping 7.62mm bullets in the direction of the infidels, he savoured the glory of his last few moments on earth.

The four-socked puppy poked his snout into the jagged bottle opening and attempted to catch the slip of paper with his tongue. He jerked his head back sharply in pain as the sharded glass opening cut his tongue slightly.

The engine roar as the bulky Warthog came around the corner and drew level with Socks startled him, and he looked up nervously to find the source of the terrifying noise.

The explosion was less than fifty feet from him and the blast wave knocked the puppy to the ground. The petrifying noise was deafening, and he yelped in pain as hot fragments of metal rained down around and on him.

Survival instincts took over and the pup turned tail and scampered away. Fast. His legs had never run like this before as he bounded across the rough ground, dodging discarded bottles and plastic containers bleached clean by the desert sun. He was seeking the shelter of his former family home, back up the incline, the search for food but a distant memory.

The top gunner of the second armoured Warthog was as nervous as hell. With only a week under his belt on the ground in Afghanistan, he had only just finished the compulsory in-country training that every soldier arriving in Afghanistan had to undergo.

Deploying to Afghanistan, he realised now, he had been full of false bravado, talking up the fight with the Taliban when they had all been in the pub back in Aldershot, glasses raised aloft in mock celebration of an easy tour of duty bagging the bad guys. It had been as if they were all bullet-proof, and family and friends were worrying for no good reason.

But, right now, there on the ground for real, with the chill desert air on his face as the Warthog accelerated along the straight section of road, he did not feel ready for this first foray into bandit country.

The reality of being in harm's way did not live up to his perception of the hero's war he had dreamt of.

Joining the army at eighteen had been his one and only focus but recruit training, as tough as it was, had not prepared him for the mental anguish of his first-ever live patrol. During training, it had been easy to dodge an 'enemy' who was firing blanks.

All he knew for sure now was that he definitely did not want to die.

He tapped the heavy, ballistic body-armour plate attached to his chest and tightened the chin strap on his combat helmet. It was some reassurance, but not enough. The issued Oakley goggles he wore ensured he would not continually wince and blink as the dirt and dust billowing out from the lead vehicle peppered his face as he scanned his 360-degree field of view for any signs of movement. Manning the mounted, heavy-duty .50 calibre machine gun gave him some crumb of reassurance: a single bullet from that bad-ass weapon could punch a football-sized hole through a car door.

They had been on patrol for exactly thirty minutes when the lead patrol vehicle was struck by a Taliban rocket.

The surprised soldier saw the impact from the corner of his eye, for a second watching helplessly as the lead vehicle was enveloped in a ballooning cloud of smoke.

'Ambush LEFT!' screamed a voice through the intercom and into the headphones he wore over his left ear. As if he needed to be told.

The top gunner's eyes flicked upwards to watch a second rocket streak dangerously close to them, only to disappear harmlessly into the distance.

There was no time to dwell on the close call. That could wait until later. Training kicked in.

Every boring, repetitive moment of weapons-drill training back in England suddenly took on new meaning as, without hesitation, all of his prevailing anxieties vanished and his booted right foot stamped down on the turret swivel mechanism pad. The gears strained as the turret-mounted machine gun swung round to his left as he grabbed the large cocking handle to force the first .50 calibre shell of the belt of ammo into the heavily oiled chamber.

The perpetrators of the rocket attacks were in plain view and charging down a slight incline directly towards his vehicle.

The novice soldier did not hesitate.

With one fluid motion he flicked off the heavy weapon's safety catch and engaged the target, the heavy *thud thud thud* obscuring the background chatter in his radio headpiece as the vehicle commander called in the 'Troops in contact' report.

The battle was over as quickly as it had started, and was nearly all one-sided.

Many days after the ambush, during the quiet hours safely back at the patrol base within Kandahar airfield, the now not-so-wet-behind-the-ears soldier – a seasoned vet compared to the newly arriving troops at the airfield – would struggle to put the attack into context. The scenes from the ambush, the close call with the second rocket-propelled grenade, and his own actions in ending someone's life continued to play out time and time again for the young man.

He would replay the images of the .50 calibre bullets striking their intended targets as if he was watching a DVD, the vivid colours flashing through his brain, the ricochets blasting skyward as the bullets from his heavy machine gun had torn into the rock-strewn desert and everything else, for that matter, which was in their way.

And he had no idea if his brain was playing tricks on him when, just for a brief second, he recalled an image of a skinny little pup wearing white socks standing out in the open before a cloud of death and destruction blanketed the scene.

chapter 2

Four White Socks

Socks ran as fast as his short legs would carry him, his skinny tail waving madly behind. His large ears flapped like useless wings from some wacky cartoon character as he wove his way around thousand-year-old rock rubble to stay on course to reach his destination. With his grubby white chest and his newly developed dark grey mane he looked, for a little fella, like a lion of sorts.

But a small one. A miniature lion of Kandahar.

Socks was excited. Food, as you would expect for any feral dog, always made Socks excited. But no matter how excited he was, he knew to stop suddenly as he approached the edge of the road, survival instincts on full alert.

Socks knew that the stretch of flat, black road that smelt of diesel fumes was a very dangerous place for a young dog like him. Lorries and cars spewed out black clouds of exhaust as they raced back and forth, horns blaring as impatient drivers attempted to overtake rusting lorries piled high with red clay bricks, before an oncoming faded green passenger bus, which had long ago crammed too many passengers on-board, thankfully called time on the crazy manoeuvre.

17

Socks just had to get across that road – but it reminded him of something . . .

There had been a loud and startling explosion, and a man in dirt-streaked clothing had charged down the hill towards the chunky metal vehicles that Socks had been attempting to scamper away from.

The dark, bearded man had almost squashed Socks as the young pup darted between the running man's feet.

The armoured vehicles on the road had stopped at the noise of the first loud bang, when red-hot fire had been unleashed in the direction of the terrified pup, including frag-ments of jagged rock that made a terrifying, ripping noise as they whizzed in all directions. One or two smaller shards of rock had left a painful burn as they struck the frightened youngster, drawing blood that had instantly matted into his brindle-coloured coat.

As Socks had mounted a large boulder, he had turned quickly to see if he had escaped the vicious maelstrom that seemed to be chasing him up the incline. Just as the storm of metal and shards of rock had enclosed him, he had seen a figure on top of one of those steel vehicles directing the red fire directly at him.

His look had lasted a mere fraction of a second as Socks, traumatised and in pain, was blown off backwards from the top of the boulder to land head-first in a heap on the ground. Dazed and without dusting himself off, he had hastily crammed himself into a gap formed by three large rocks. It had been a perfect pup-sized shelter. The noise all round him had been thunderously loud and he had tried to scrabble more deeply into the safety of the shelter.

As the thunder had finally died down, it had been replaced by many minutes of screaming and yelling voices, and people clambering all over the ground in front of him before, at last, his surroundings had fallen silent.

Socks had fallen asleep.

It was many hours before he had had the courage and had felt the pangs of hunger that had told him he should move, his skinny, undernourished body shivering from the cold of lying between the rocks for so long. The midday sun had felt warm on his back as he had craned his neck forward and arched his back in a typical puppy stretch as he readied himself for his continuous search for food.

With no wind to clear the air, there had been a lingering, burning smell, and the caustic fumes had invaded the pup's nostrils as he checked cautiously that it was safe to be exposed on the open ground once more.

Nearly a year had passed since that close call and, with his wounds having healed well, Socks had not witnessed anything like that since. He had heard dull *whump*s during the day sometimes, but they were far off in the distance and as they hadn't affected him, he had just carried on with his recces for something to eat.

Now, as he paused at the edge of the road as a bulky cargo truck trundled passed, his sole focus was his intent on crossing the road. There was an audible *clank* from a passing car's suspension as the rusting springs fought to absorb the shock as the driver failed to negotiate the shallow crater still left from the former attack. No one had yet been sent to smooth out the pit, and probably wouldn't until the whole road was due to be resurfaced – if it ever was.

Socks was a clever little soul these days. He would never know what fate had befallen his siblings – whether they had died from starvation or disease – but on finding himself on his own all that time ago, he had realised pretty much right away what was safe and what was not. Or so he assumed, anyway. *This* side of the road, barren and devoid of homesteads, had been safe for his mum to conceal his brother and sisters. She had chosen a perfect spot far from the normal, everyday activities of people. On her forages for food, she had been able to leave the pups without too much fear of them being discovered. There was no reason for any person to wander this far from the beaten track. Most avoided these wasteland areas, due to the threat from the thousands of randomly dropped landmines – a cruel and hate-filled goodbye present from the Soviets as they had fled Afghanistan – which now dangerously littered the countryside and made much of the land uninhabitable.

Socks had wisely followed his prudent mum's example and kept the old family den as his. He returned nightly to the now lonely and very empty hollow each day as darkness fell, to curl up tightly by himself and attempt to hold the coldness at bay. As sleep took hold he would kick out his short, white-tipped legs in random little jerks, his breathing coming in terse, tiny bursts as he dreamt of chasing his siblings over the desert rocks as his proud mum kept watch. He always woke up with a start, his surroundings unseen in the darkness of the night, realising that he was still alone. He would curl up even tighter and attempt to go back to a fitful sleep.

Although Socks was fairly safe from any unwanted human contact, he had also realised, very quickly, that the downside to retreating to that side of the road meant that food was either scarce or non-existent: he rarely struck lucky as he sniffed amongst the empty cartons and packaging from everyday life that had been tossed from speeding vehicles. But he *had* got lucky that day – he had sniffed out a round, slightly soggy *naan* bread at the edge of the road, no doubt accidentally dropped by a passenger struggling to eat and stay balanced in the back of a passing truck.

The hungry pup with the lion's mane had eaten well that day, hurriedly hopping between the moonscape of rocks back to his den, the delicious-tasting *naan* clamped firmly between his teeth, his wispy tail unable to conceal his anticipation at the meal to come.

But one piece of naan, however filling, hadn't kept a hungry pup satisfied for long.

Socks had to cross the road from his isolated and uninhabitable side and head for the populated areas – a treasure trove of food for a starving young pup – if he wanted to survive. It was obviously where his mum had journeyed to seek food in order to be able to provide for her demanding pups, but Socks was also extremely aware that she too had had to cross that road to search among the narrow, rubbish-strewn alleys that gave access to the sprawling compounds and houses that made up the boundary to Kandahar city.

With no municipal services as such operating in Kandahar, households abandoned their daily rubbish into the already cluttered alleyways that linked communities. Rubbish removal was the task of the many Afghans involved in the back street market recycling trade. Riding skinny-tyred bicycles with enormous hessian bags hung over the seats, young

Afghan men would clamber through the piles of rotting rubbish sorting plastic, tins and wood to load into the giant sacks attached to their bikes. Once full, these would reach to the ground as they rode away, their *salwar kameez* discoloured and reeking of sweat. Their hoarded treasure would fetch mere pence once it was sold on for the long journey back to the manufacturing powerhouses of China and Pakistan, to be processed and used once more.

It was commonplace to witness the local goat herder feeding his flock from the knee-deep mixture of rotting rubbish, fattening up the herd for the butcher's block and maximising profits. And dogs like Socks – thousands of them that lived in close proximity to the densely urbanised areas of Afghanistan – would also root through the plentiful rubbish to munch on unused potato peels, discarded rice and soggy *naan* bread. Like Socks, they would be extremely lucky if they were to find a tiny scrap of chicken, say, left attached to a picked-clean chicken bone.

And this was where Socks was now headed. To the place where people lived.

The road was busy at this time of day but not so that he would not be able to cross, the black surface always hot on the pads of his paws as he charged across. He had grown accustomed to waiting patiently for a gap between the lumbering metal monsters before leaping onto the tarmac surface and rushing headlong to the relative safety of the other side.

He knew there would be no screeching of brakes if he judged it wrong.

Once safely across on the other side, though, he was in plain sight of the people that walked along the side of the unfinished dirt service road which connected the many alleys leading from the sprawling housing compounds to the main road he had just crossed. It was an added danger.

Keeping out of sight for as long as possible, Socks would slide down the gentle incline of a barren drainage ditch which was usually choked with rubbish, waiting as it was for the rains to wash its channels clean by sending the cluttered trash back to Pakistan via the network of rivers that flowed south. He would run with his nose to the ground, sniffing for any scent of food as he continued along the side of the road, his wary eyes continually on the lookout for trouble.

When he reached the section where the drainage ditch disappeared under the road in a narrow, dark tunnel, he would push up to the lip of the ditch and, quickly checking his surroundings once more, would venture hastily across the open ground into a nearby alley.

Occasionally, as he reached the middle of the open expanse, he would sometimes stop and throw caution to the wind. Sitting on his haunches, his shaggy head craning up towards the sky, Socks would call out to his mum, the piercing howl vibrating around the high, rock-hard compound walls that marked the boundary to the human world, the long strands of his hairy coat dancing in the stiff, chill wind that would buffet the young pup as he called out.

With his ears pricked up like antennas searching for a radio signal, he would sit attentively and wait. Vulnerable and alone in the open.

But he would call for her again. Just in case his mum, with her dirt-stained face and gentle nurturing ways, was lost and could hear him.

The silence in those moments was deafening. Socks would strain to hear a reply – a knowing bark that she was on her way back to him; a nearby whimper of pleasure as she rounded the corner and saw him.

But she never replied.

Socks would wait just a few minutes more, oblivious to his surroundings but then growing evermore aware of the close proximity of the people as they hurried passed along the edge of the unfinished road, eager to reach their destination and shelter from the cold wind.

Finally, he would trot off to continue his vital mission for food, sadness heavy in his heart.

The old lady smiled. Her wrinkled and weather-worn face, with her piercing blue eyes, showed no signs of fear. Her black, tattered, ankle-length dress, faded from years of wearing, fluttered gently around her feet in the early evening breeze.

'*Shomâ az kojâ hastêð?*' She spoke softly as she asked the scared-looking pup, its tail tucked firmly between its hind legs, where it was from.

'*Shomâ chanð sâi ðârêð?*' She hoped her voice was soothing as she asked him how old he was.

She had always adored puppies, with their innocent little faces all mushed up during their first days of life. As a child she had longed for a puppy to be her companion, but her strict Muslim father had never allowed it. Sneaking scraps of food from the house to carefully lay out for the neighbourhood strays had been her only relief, and she had known that she risked unleashing her father's wrath if she was caught. He toiled long hours and in the harshest of weathers to put food on the family's table, and would not have taken kindly to it benefiting the local dog population, however much in need of it she thought they were.

When she had been married, to a man her father had chosen, it had become easier to continue her passion for looking after strays. As was traditionally required, she had moved to live with her husband's family, which had been a blessing in disguise as far as her secret hobby was concerned.

Her husband had been a builder by trade and in charge of his own company, too. He had proudly built a spacious family home, in a more secluded area of Kandahar, high, sturdy, mud-built walls painted white that were now faded and peeling, surrounded the home from prying eyes.

With both his parents frail and unable to move too far from the main living room, she had taken over in the kitchen and had thereby been free to do as she pleased, as long as his parent's needs were seen to. She had no reason to leave their well-equipped compound – not that she could without her husband to accompany her, as the law dictated. But that didn't bother her too much. It was all she had ever known.

Squirreling away food for the local street dogs was a simple task, and placing it outside the compound's rear gate during her husband's parents' afternoon nap had become the highlight of her usually mundane day.

Many years later, when her husband's parents had passed and their only child, a daughter, Mahila, had been married off, the now old lady had, by and large, the whole day alone to occupy herself. But, happily, for the first time in over six decades, she had a personal, four-legged companion.

Every day, just as the sun floated over the highest point of the tall minaret of the nearby mosque, its four corners mounted with large blue speakers to remind everyone within earshot when they were being called to prayer, she would wait patiently for the white-socked puppy – an inquisitive little character, no more than five or six months old, with his distinct orange-brown eyes taking in everything around him.

He would venture carefully towards the bowl of fresh food that she tenderly laid out of sight behind a rusting car, long abandoned and forgotten in the dead-end alley that wove its way past the rear gate at which she now stood. The weary pup would sniff the cooling bowl of rice and, when satisfied all was well, would tuck in heartily, never really stopping to chew the food properly, gulping it down as if he had not eaten in days. And she would smile to herself when the pup discovered the nugget-sized piece of chicken or goat she had hidden carefully under the freshly prepared rice mound.

It had taken quite a few visits before the pup had stopped backing off as soon as he had finished licking the plate clean – almost returning it to its kitchen shelf glory each time – but the old lady had been patient. She had begun to hide a further piece of meat in her right hand and offer it to the youngster when he had finished the plateful, her arm outstretched, trying not to scare away her new friend.

'*Morgh mêkhâhêd?*' More chicken? she asked calmly, as the pup weighed up his choices.

He was not going to say no.

As time progressed, once he had chased the last piece of rice around the plate, he would sit boldly and patiently upright in front of his host, his proud bleached-white patch of chest on full display as he waited for the final chicken titbit.

The old lady marvelled at how gently the quickly growing dog would nibble the chicken from her fingers. He never snatched, his fluffy grey tail wagging excitedly behind him as he gobbled up the tasty morsel.

'*Khalâs*,' she would say, as she indicated that the chicken was finished, presenting her open palms for the curious youngster to examine. Without subtly changing her position, she would stretch out her arm in an attempt to stroke the grey mop of hair that sprouted in all directions from the dog's head.

At first the wary dog would bound backwards, just out of reach, his tail down as he tried to work out her intentions, his head cocked to one side as he waited for the old lady's next move. Hoping, of course, that it would involve more food.

But he would not run off. He would stay and wait.

'*Naan, nê.*' She would shake her head slowly as she quietly told him there was no more food.

She had stumbled upon the young, white-socked puppy by accident. He had been sniffing around the rusted shell of the car dumped by her compound's rear gate, the important recyclable items stripped clean long ago. Looking alone and vulnerable, she had shooed away the larger dogs that had been following him up the alley.

His proud, fluffy tail had wagged excitedly as she had placed the bowl on the ground. She hadn't thought she would see him again but the inquisitive youngster had been back the following day and then the day after that, too.

As the weeks progressed, and their short moments together merged into one, Socks gradually began to let the old lady gently ruffle the top of his head. The woman's slender fingers were calming and hypnotic to the young stray – it reminded him of his mother cleaning and licking him as she had once done, long ago. The old lady loved how soft and fine his hair felt. Gently caressing one of his long, fluffy ears, she could feel the dog pressing his head against her palm, and she smiled happily, knowing that when she stopped, the once wary dog would actually inch closer to her and gently nudge her hand with the side of its head, demanding that she continue. She was happy to oblige.

She couldn't help but smile when Socks, now almost a year old as far as she could tell, lay down right in front of her when the food ritual had finished, slightly rolled onto his back and lifted his leg high into the air so his belly was on full view, clearly hoping she would indulge him with a belly rub.

The old lady delighted in complying with her four-legged buddy's request, crouching lower as she rubbed his white-coated belly.

Socks relaxed. Right then, he had not a care in the world. Humans, it seemed to him, were not that bad.

chapter 3

The Wheelbarrow

The young British troop sergeant was not totally sure what he was meant to do.

'Hello Zero, this is Two Zero Charlie. I have a situation here. Over,' was all he could think to say into the plastic mike strapped snugly to the left side of his sweat-streaked face. He used the usual call-sign indicators so that command would know who was calling, but if anyone was listening in who shouldn't be, then he was just another number.

The last few hours of continuous crawling alongside the sun-baked mud walls of compounds, used as cover during his troop's search for a very persistent Taliban sniper, had left them all tired, the sergeant's clothing damp from the physical exertion of throwing himself to the ground to take cover, followed by the struggle to jump to his feet with the full combat load he carried on his back, only to charge forward again as they cleared the next piece of ground. The sniper had kept them busy firing his, thankfully, not so well aimed shots in their direction. The troop machine gunner had returned the favour, allowing the sergeant and the rest of his men to move closer to the sniper's position under the cover of the supporting fire.

He felt a chill as the post-battle euphoria waned – the sniper's position had been neutralised. The sergeant took a look
down the line of the drainage ditch that paralleled the track
that was their limit of advance. Having reached the linear
feature, his company of Royal Marines had been ordered to
go to ground to await further direction from headquarters.

The opportunity to rest had been appreciated. His young
Marines had remembered their training well and were
spaced out evenly, crouching in the cover the shallow ditch
provided, alternating their arcs to provide cover as they took
the opportunity to down some lukewarm water from their
combat packs.

Their pre-deployment training had been extremely
thorough, even down to actual former Afghan nationals,
now residents in the UK, acting as Afghan villagers in a
mock-up Helmand village that had been built on Salisbury
Plain. It had been amusing to them at the time that the
majority of drivers hurtling along the A303 trunk road
had not had the foggiest idea that a battle for Afghanistan
was happening just three corn fields away. Presenting the
soldiers with the experience of forcibly entering a Pashtun
village during a hunt for a Taliban fighter, whilst dealing
with the painful delay in communications associated with
everything being looped through an interpreter, often led
the commanders to re-assess their battle plans. Enthusiastic
acting had actually come to blows at one point as a pretend
village elder had taken offence to being told to, 'Bugger
off back to Afghan' by one of the Marines, who had failed
to appreciate the fact that he was meant to use the interpreter to urge the elder's family to vacate their pretend
house. The stand-out moment had been when the directing staff had had to intervene to restrain the windmilling

arms and fists – it turned out that the 'elder' actually spoke with a stronger Brummie accent than the fresh-faced private.

However, this current real life situation was not funny.

'Hello Zero, this is Two Zero Charlie. Seriously need a heads-up here, please. Over.' After another minute's wait, the young sergeant – two months into his first deployment to this unforgiving country – realised that he could not wait any more for a response from Zero.

He would have to make a call on this one.

He stood up from his cramped fire position off to the side of the featureless dirt track that doubled as a main road in this rural part of Afghanistan, his knees aching immediately as the bulk of the combat pack he carried came to bear, and quickly adjusted the position of the cumbersome helmet on his head – even after two, long months in Afghanistan, there was just nothing anyone could do to make the bloody thing wearable for any length of time. Then he moved with as much authority as he could muster to the middle of the dusty track and held up his left hand in the universal 'stop' signal.

His right hand remained firmly on the pistol grip of his automatic rifle, index finger stretched across the trigger guard.

'Got you covered, sergeant,' a voice whispered in his ear over the troop radio net. He realised suddenly how reassuring it was to know that the owner of that voice had a sniper rifle trained protectively in his direction.

'Stop,' he shouted, as he emphasised the stop signal with his left hand, his outstretched combat-gloved hand clear for all to see.

A group of village elders, their pointed, greying beards hanging luxuriantly from the lower halves of extremely weather-beaten faces, their feet – calloused and dirt-covered from having to walk everywhere – in sandaled footwear the sergeant actually deemed to be extremely inappropriate for the landscape of Afghanistan, shuffled to a halt.

He quickly did a headcount.

Eight old men, in total.

'Now what?' the concerned sergeant thought out loud. He knew the unit interpreter was engaged with the command cell. He was on his own for this one. He only knew how to say, 'Put your hands up' in the local dialect, but he had already realised that on this occasion that particular phrase would not come in handy. He made a mental note to actually bother to learn some more words.

The eight elders ranged in years from old to ancient, the sergeant observing that not one appeared able to stand upright properly, their backs crooked with the passing of the years. The shabby, thin, traditional Afghan clothing seemingly scant protection against the harsh winds that the southern Afghan winter had to offer. Only one wore a coat of any description – a black padded one.

'How the hell have they managed to walk here?' the sergeant asked himself as he tried to recall map details in his head. It had to be three miles from the nearest village to his present location, along the isolated track on which they were all now standing.

But they had walked here. And they were in front of him.

The youngest-looking of the group – at a push, the sergeant

deemed him to be at least sixty years old – was hidden towards the rear of the huddle, and was pushing a wheelbarrow, a faded blue tarp covering its contents. He seemed relieved that he could rest now.

'Weapons?' the sergeant said to himself, as he gave the group another once-over, without trying to be obvious. But then he resisted the urge to smile as he imagined this group of elderly Afghans trying to launch a surprise attack on him.

He figured they would need at least two minutes just to get warmed up.

He also knew that by now the sniper, who was lying hidden amongst rocky tundra some 300 feet away, would also have assessed each elder through the high-magnification telescopic sight attached to the body of his weapon. If he had been the slightest bit concerned that a weapon was being concealed, then the sergeant knew he would have known about it by now.

The old man at the head of the group, his stern face show-ing the years of hard toil required to live a long life in Afghanistan, stepped forward and walked towards the sergeant, his fist-length, wispy beard a clean white. A pale brown Afghan head scarf was wrapped tightly around the Afghan elder's shoulders, resting on the shoulder pads of his faded suit jacket. He was tall – at least six foot. A black turban sat tightly on his head.

'Peace be upon you, my friend.'

The phrase, in almost perfect English, startled the sergeant. He most definitely had not been expecting that.

The elder extended his right hand in the timeless gesture of a handshake.

'And peace be upon you as well,' the sergeant replied, a look of surprise still etched across his face as he firmly shook the old man's cold hand before regaining the grip on his rifle.

'I am English teacher,' the elder proudly explained, his yellow-stained teeth evident as a broad grin broke the stern features. But the grin disappeared as quickly as it had appeared as he continued before the sergeant could respond. 'My good friend here' – the elder turned to indicate a much older gentleman whose dark face, wrinkled and tanned by the desert sun, spoke of a lifetime of work in the fields – 'would like you to know that his only son has just been killed by your aeroplane.'

Upon hearing that, the sergeant's mind began racing, unsure of what to say. He had to stop himself blurting out that it was not his aeroplane, but he checked himself to gather his thoughts. It was not the time to argue semantics.

Now, the huddle of elders parted quietly and the Afghan in control of the wheelbarrow pushed his charge forward. He lowered the barrow gently to the ground just in front of the soldier, and stepped back. Without warning, the English teacher grabbed the top corner of the faded tarp and pulled it back.

The sergeant stared at what was underneath.

The body of the old Afghan's child had been placed as carefully as anyone could place a dead child in a wheelbarrow. His face was dirt-streaked and pale, his eyes closed. Maybe ten years old – no more, the sergeant guessed. Thick towels that had since become soaked through with blood were wrapped tightly around the child's stomach.

The sergeant had been in a similar situation in Iraq, involving a government-laid landmine and a group of children, but the suddenness of this presentation had caught him off-guard. He lowered his head. He didn't need to look any more. No training could prepare anybody to see something like that.

For it to be a young child as well, his life cruelly extinguished in somebody else's war.

Realising in that moment that there was no threat from the group of mourning men, the sergeant let his rifle hang down by his side as he raised his right hand to cover his heart, feeling as though he had suddenly aged. He looked the old man squarely in the eyes and simply said, 'Sorry.'

It was easy to summarise what had happened. An Apache attack helicopter, the most powerful and deadly of all the assets the military could bring to bear, had been tasked to engage with the enemy firing point. It had done so with devastating effectiveness. Its missiles had destroyed buildings in the blink of an eye, the mushroom cloud from the heated air rising several hundred feet into the clear blue sky on the eastern edge of the village.

And while the Taliban fighters might have been no more, the child had been hit by shrapnel from the resulting explosions.

Why the child had been near to the scene of the fighting he had no idea.

The English teacher was staring intently at the sergeant. 'You pay him for this loss.' It was a statement of fact rather than a question.

The first time the sergeant had heard this Afghan demand for compensation so soon after a relative's death, he had felt revulsion. The child had not even been buried yet. But the more he learnt about Afghan culture, especially in the Taliban heartlands of southern Afghanistan, the more he understood that out there, a son was everything to an Afghan family. A young boy was sent out to work as soon as he could walk – he had seen with his own eyes six-year-olds working tired-look-ing donkeys resigned to their fate as a life-long workhorse as it carried water to the next village. Or the children were sent to the work the streets, washing car windows as traffic crawled along at a snail's pace in the congested and very polluted streets of Kabul. It was a dangerous occupation for children: the cars never stopped as they cleaned the windows.

When old age took away the head of the family's ability to keep his family, then the sons would take on that responsibil-ity. The son's duty was to keep the family name and traditions alive. Now, the grieving father – far too old to be having any more children – was standing on a barren track with one of his sons lying dead in a wheelbarrow.

Word travelled fast and the conflict-weary Afghans knew that the western troops paid compensation. Compensation the father would need if he was to continue feeding his family when he became too frail to do so – that point in the old man's life was not too far in the future, the sergeant reckoned. And while the Afghans' complete belief in their religion meant death was not to be feared, all Afghans, save for the minority fanatical types, were keen to live as long as they possibly could, of course. And the living most definitely still had to eat.

Thankfully, for this scenario – which he realised he had never actually thought would happen – the sergeant had been briefed.

There was even a military drill for this eventuality.

He reached deep into the map pocket on the thigh of his combat trousers and pulled out his olive-drab notebook. He fished through it until he found the few, loose pieces of paper carefully folded to fit inside the notebook.

The brightly drawn cartoon characters, depicting an Afghan family, which illustrated the printed material, somehow did not do the seriousness of the leaflet's message justice. The characters explained what an Afghan man should do in this very circumstance. The only written item on the paper was a phone number in Pashtun, next to a cartoon Afghan man holding a phone to his ear.

'Make a call to this number.' The sergeant offered the leaflet to the English teacher. Even in these remote parts of Afghanistan, nearly every male had a mobile phone.

The English teacher nodded and, refolding the leaflet without ceremony, placed it inside a hidden pocket in his *salwar kameez* shirt pocket. 'And this man's son was injured,' he said, as he pointed to a shorter gentleman, his greying beard close-cropped.

The old man's wrinkled, darkly tanned face stared back at the sergeant. Nodding slowly, his open mouth revealed a gap where his two front teeth should have been. His dark suit jacket was faded and worn and completely contrasted with the white *salwar kameez* trousers he wore, while his black leather shoes had most definitely seen better days. The sergeant had already noticed he did not wear socks.

The school teacher continued: 'The Americans took his injured son away in a helicopter. Where?' The proud smile of earlier had long since vanished.

The sergeant had been too busy ensuring that his soldiers were all uninjured and arranging for an ammunition resupply, to take much notice of any other non-combatant events going on around them, but he could recall looking up and watching briefly an American Blackhawk helicopter silhouetted against the impossibly blue sky, circling as if it meant to land. He couldn't remember seeing it again, but then the company sergeant major had been on his arse for the ammunition and casualty report. And you didn't disappoint the company sergeant major.

The nearest airbase was Kandahar military airfield, at least a day's drive north. The main hub for all coalition troops operating in the south of the country, it was home to a hospital that catered for both injured coalition military and Afghan civilians.

'Kandahar airfield,' the sergeant replied, pointing to the north.

The English teacher said, 'Thank you. May God be with you,' as he turned and beckoned, both arms outstretched, for the group of elders to turn around and go back the way they had come.

As one they turned and shuffled off along the track, a small cloud of dust trailing behind from the specks of gravel and dirt flicked up by their sandaled feet, the wheelbarrow pusher following on behind.

The sergeant took a breath and let out a long sigh. His radio headset crackled into life.

'Two Zero Charlie, this is Zero. Sorry for the delay. What's the problem? Over.'

The sergeant turned away from the sight of the elders as they walked off into the distance, and moved to take up his former fire position, tucked off to the side of the track, to continue the wait for further orders.

He pressed the transmit button on his radio controller. 'Two Zero Charlie – all dealt with. Nothing to report. Out.'

chapter 4

Aussie

'Well, that didn't go quite as well as we had planned,' the Australian Federal Police officer exclaimed to nobody in particular with a wry smile as she shook her head. Her brown hair was tied in a ponytail and pulled back tightly under her blue police cap, the Australian Federal Police badge front and centre on her well-worn headgear.

The chill of the night had disappeared as the sun rose into the cold, blue sky, high above the top of the triple-stacked HESCO bollards – boxed metal fencing that, when filled with dirt, provided a solid bullet-stopper to make the outer perimeter walls to Kandahar airfield.

It was turning out to be quite a pleasant morning, she realised, unless for your own protection you were forced to walk around with the cumbersome, standard-issue body armour on all the time. The added addition of the desert camouflage combat helmet strapped firmly to one's head didn't help much either, especially where the leather chin patch cupped the chin. But, thankfully, for this training exercise she could relax slightly and just have her helmet to hand.

In front of her, six young Afghan National Police in their thick blue uniforms, devoid of insignia except for a single strip of colour over their left chest pocket which identified them as trainees, were currently crouching down, huddled together, facing inwards in vocal heated debate, their rich Pashtun dialect incomprehensible to the young Aussie police-woman, their unloaded rifles lying uselessly next to them.

The vehicle checkpoint they were meant to be manning was now completely unattended. A battered Toyota Corolla, painted in the distinct sickly yellow that identified it as an Afghan taxi, waited patiently for the trainees to come to an agreement. There was no one to stop it from actually driving away along the dirt track.

Danielle sighed to herself. Just like most coalition troops attempting to train Afghan recruits she would probably be there for some time.

The first thing any soldier sent to serve in Afghanistan noticed was that more or less everybody drove a Corolla.

The country was the epicentre for Corollas. The Afghan love affair with the Corolla was legendary and, to an outsider, somewhat bizarre. Hundreds of Corollas were registered every single day in Kabul alone. Most young men would spend hours cleaning and decorating their Corolla, often paying far too much of their meagre salaries having westernised slogans sten-cilled across the rear windscreen, mostly with the English grammar leaving a lot to be desired. Danielle smiled to herself as she thought of one she had seen just the other day: 'Danger, Danger, love is killer!' in bright yellow capitals.

Not many considered that Afghan men fell in love judging from the traditions of arranged marriages.

The car's spare-parts business was a roaring mini-economy, judging by the corrugated shacks that adorned the side of every road, where salvaged parts were polished with loving care and hung from every available space to reel in the trade. The fact that you could not drive more than 100 yards in any direction along the many unpaved roads without hearing the *crunch* of a car's suspension as it failed to negotiate the prolific potholes that besieged Afghan roads ensured that business was always booming.

She glanced across at the driver of the unmoving Corolla through the unwashed windscreen. His short-cropped blond hair and dark sunglasses instantly gave him away as a westerner, while his large frame and bulky combat clothing gave him the impression of being shoehorned into the driver's seat, the steering wheel almost pressing against his ballistic chest plate. As like most western troops depolyed to Afghanistan, the Aussie Police Officer lived for his morning gym workout, and the front seat of a Corolla would have looked cramped with him just sitting in his gym gear.

Her Aussie compatriot looked up from tapping his fingers on the pitted dashboard and smirked as he saw her eyeballing him. He fought to crane his head out of the driver's side window so that he could yell across to her in his strong Australian twang: 'Danielle, what the hell are they doing now?'

This was the second training run that had ended in farce. No matter how many times they ran through the drills there was always something. And just of late, it was tribal tension. Mustafa, the towering bearded trainee from a *Hazara* family in Kabul, was not happy at being told what to do by Toofan, the fresh-faced younger man from Herat who had been put in charge for this particular exercise and whose family were *Tajik*. Afghanistan was a constant powder keg of various ethnic groups struggling to gain or hold on to power, even down to the individual Police recruits. How the Afghan

Government functioned with all the various ethnic tribal disputes was a miracle really.

Frustrating really did not cut it as a suitable adjective to describe attempting to train the Afghan police.

The Australian Federal Police had been in Afghanistan since 2009 to deliver training to segments of the Afghan National Police over a two-year period, in co-ordination with other coalition police forces. With over 500 Afghan policemen passed fit for duty, the Australian trainers could be justifiably certain that they had contributed to enforcing the rule of law in a country fabled for its lawless ways.

Right now though, it would be stupid to assume that these six would be adding to that achievement any time soon.

Danielle shrugged her shoulders and turned to look for Najeebullah, her not-overly-enthusiastic translator. It took her a couple of moments to spot him – he was crouched to the side of the vehicle checkpoint, in the shade of a transport shipping container that currently doubled up as the police store room.

'Najeeb!' she yelled across at him. He was engrossed with his mobile phone, oblivious to the raised voices emanating from the huddled Afghans.

He frowned back at her, as if he was annoyed that she had disturbed his concentration.

'Hellooo?' she stressed the word. 'They have stopped again.' And she indicated for him to intervene. Najeeb made a great show of standing up and sauntering over to the trainees. There were not many Afghan men happy taking orders from a woman of any nationality.

Bored of waiting, her fellow Aussie started up the Corolla's engine and slammed it into first gear as he sped out of the checkpoint to drive around for the next run-through, the rear tyres spitting gravel skyward as they struggled for traction.

She was always envious to see somebody else having the opportunity to drive the car. It beat the hell out of standing watching Afghans argue. Constantly. She turned to look out over towards the sun-soaked, distant mountains. She knew it would take Najeeb at least five minutes to straighten out the drama, whatever it was this time.

It had been a fairly surreal affair coming to Afghanistan in the middle of a war that showed no signs of either side being able to win; not to fight, but to turn mostly uneducated men into the bastion of a democratic society – a police force.

Most westerners who served in Afghanistan, would try to understand the culture and mentality of these young Afghan men. Nearly all admired their commitment and determination to see change in their country – the Taliban had long ago declared all Afghan policemen to be the puppets of a western-backed government and therefore legitimate targets. Some of these young men would not be able to go back to their home villages for many years once word had spread that they had joined the ranks of the ANP.

Folks back home would have a hard time understanding that. The smarter Afghans left home stating their intentions of sourcing manual labour in Kabul or further afield. As long as their monthly 'keep' money was sent home to their parents and family, then nobody was any the wiser.

During those early months of nervousness, the Australian Police had settled into the daily unpredictability of life on Kandahar airfield, and had taken comfort – as did everybody else – at being surrounded by the formidable coalition war machine, with all of its sophisticated technology and support that could be brought to bear at a moment's notice. But as the months had dragged on, most would begin to question and maybe even doubt the effectiveness of it all. A guerrilla force that basically wore sandals and relied on mobile phones for communications was still pretty much actively directing the course of the war in the south – the 107mm rockets they lobbed into the airbase from time to time, causing all not on essential sentry duty to run for the security of the concrete mortar shelters dotted protectively around base, was proof enough of that.

She flicked the police cap from her head and ruffled her hair. The sensation of cool air around her scalp was refreshing, and she waited for as long as she could before placing her cap firmly back on her head. Orders dictated that women were to wear headgear lest they upset the local Afghan men. Wearing a baseball cap was the easy option compared to the poor Afghan women forced to live their lives in a *burka*. Besides, it was most definitely preferable to the weighty combat helmet currently strapped to her waist. When that cumbersome Kevlar bucket went on her head, then she was in trouble.

Working day in, day out with these trainees would take its toll on anybody. It would take the hardest of souls to keep a sense of humour whilst repeating a simple training exercise that they should have nailed yesterday and had most definitely not carried through into the next morning. Would anybody miss training the Afghan police when that long-awaited flight back home finally came calling? But for Danielle she was bound to feel a tinge of sadness as she thought about the completely unofficial mission she had given herself, and how much she would miss it when her time in Afghanistan finally came to a close.

Without any fanfare, and whilst doing her best to stay below the radar of the base's higher command, she had become a dog rescuer of sorts to the local strays that scavenged outside the perimeter fence of Kandahar airfield.

From her vantage point, within the safety of the base, she witnessed the plight of the feral dogs on their never-ending mission to find the next meagre scrap of food. A miserable cycle that never changed. Like anybody who loved dogs, it was at times just too painful for her to watch the scrawny young strays, with no hope for a loving home, desperately trying to survive in a country where even the people had the odds stacked against them; strays that, as far as it went, had nobody to look out for them. Until Danielle had decided to try and make a difference.

To begin with, when she had started trying to help them, she had worried about what would happen to the strays when she was finally sent home to Australia: there was no one else to take on the role she had started. She could only affect for better the here and now and so, it was best to do whatever it took to make as much difference as possible to as many dogs as she could whilst she was in Afghanistan.

It had started out at entry checkpoint five, one of the many coalition tactical positions that made up the secure perimeter to defend the commercial entrance to Kandahar airfield. The heavily sandbagged position was a focal point for 'locally directed non-compliance' at what many saw as the unlawful intervention in Afghanistan by the westerners.

Soldiers at the checkpoint had definitely been in amongst the thick of it, from angered locals throwing rocks, to the more accurate small-arms attacks which had also included, at times, thankfully inaccurate rocket-propelled grenades. The lads had their hands full in providing the first line of defence.

This opposition to westerners was not really too surprising for anybody stationed in southern Afghanistan. Kandahar, the second biggest city in Afghanistan and without doubt the epicentre of opium production, was the spiritual home of Mullah Omar and so, by association, the Taliban.

In 1996 Mullah Omar, with his bestowed grand title of 'Commander of the Faithful' was a legend to many Pashtuns in the predominantly tribal provinces of south Afghanistan. The *mullah*, a madrasa teacher who had fought the Soviets, held legendary status from the time he had, as the story went, led thirty men armed with only sixteen rifles to free two young girls who had been kidnapped and abused by a local warlord. Freeing the girls, the *mullah* had sent a very public warning to deter others from attempting a vile act like that again: he had hung the warlord. His rise to a senior position within the Taliban regime had been swift.

Mullah Omar very rarely left the safety of his beloved Kandahar and those loyal to him rallied to his cause when he declared his contempt for the westerners now occupying Afghanistan.

The entry checkpoint had been a popular target for that contempt.

Positive distractions for those alert and scanning for signs of a Taliban attack were few and far between. When not manning the heavy machine gun positions or fully booted and spurred to provide the vehicle search parties, the lads were tucked away in less than savoury bunkers, trying to catch up on much needed sleep or scribbling a hastily written letter back home on 'blueys' – the blue A4 sheet of paper that folds neatly into its own envelope, which would be mailed home on the next resupply run.

'Lady', however, was one such positive distraction. She had arrived during January 2011. The slightly chubby-looking, golden-coated mongrel dog, with a band of dirty white around her muzzle that rose up between her piercing eyes to disappear in a thin streak over the back of her head, had darted into entry checkpoint five one day, her fur matted with blood.

The on-duty soldiers had spotted the stray dog earlier through the telescopic scope of their assault rifles as they had watched the flow of daily life drift by their arcs. One soldier had focused on the stray dog, the cross-hairs of his scope following the rotund dog's outline as it sniffed around a few discarded empty cans, the lingering smell of food long-since eaten its only reward.

After several minutes of hunting, and after all hopes of finding something edible had been dashed, the dog, when it had satisfied itself that the particular spot in question, devoid of litter and grass, was safely away from human interaction or other feral dogs, had walked round in tight circles on the small verge, before dropping to the dusty ground. With its body half propped against the side of a long-ago abandoned, mud-walled compound, the dog made sure it was curled head to toe tightly, as it seemingly made the most of the winter sun's warming rays to catch up on some sleep.

The sentry position overlooking the cleared and open approaches to the checkpoint was a cold place to undertake the two hours of constant vigilance required of every sentry duty, as the sun never penetrated the doubled-layered sandbags that surrounded each fire position that was mounted on top of each corner of the HESCO earth-filled defensive barriers that formed the walls of the checkpoint. The barriers stacked two high, made an immovable wall around the checkpoint that was impenetrable to small arms fire and rocket propelled grenade attack. A flimsy wooden frame supported a single panelled sheet of wood that acted as a roof of sorts above each sentry position keeping the worst of the weather at bay but also putting paid to any direct sunlight that would take the edge off the cold. And the constant chill was working wonders in focusing the concentration of the soldier currently on watch, who adjusted his position ever so slightly to watch a blue-*burka*-clad woman carrying a brightly dressed infant in one arm, counterbalanced by a substantial-sized plastic yellow container in the other hand.

The soldier assumed it contained water. Most houses didn't have access to running water. He wondered about her age and what she looked like under the all-encompassing body dress that all women in the Taliban-influenced provinces wore. For some unknown reason, it pained him that he would never know either answer.

The soldier struggled to comprehend the reasoning behind the Taliban's treatment of women. During pre-deployment training, it had been explained that the Taliban believed a woman's sole purpose in life was to provide a man with an all-important son, and the more boys she gave birth to, the better. The soldier, along with his comrades, had burst out laughing when they had learned that a man could take as many as four wives if he could support them all equally – he struggled just trying to keep his one girlfriend happy. He couldn't imagine how anyone could keep four women happy all at the same time. Complete madness.

He focused back on the woman and her child. The *burka* was designed to disguise the female form, as it was the Taliban belief that any woman away from the home would tempt other men into sexual relations. Hence the all-covering *burka* to prevent any men who came to glance upon a woman in the streets from becoming aroused.

To the soldier, it was the philosophy of people left idling in centuries-old traditions that had no place in the twenty-first century.

Just then, sudden sounds of distressed barking – obviously a dog in pain – broke the relative calm of the moment. The soldier instantly refocused on the area that the dog had settled in earlier.

The cross-hairs of his rifle, its olive-drab barrel the only visible sign that anybody occupied the sentry position, sighted on the large dog bolting from its former resting position as a barrage of fist-sized rocks rained down on it. The soldier looked on, pulse racing with shock as the defenceless dog was knocked sideways as two of the larger thrown rocks connected with it.

Without having to think about it, his upper body and the rifle moved as one, as if the weapon was an extra appendage growing from his shoulder, as he scanned back towards the source of the attack, leaving the fleeing dog to continue its escape.

Afghan teens, just kids really, dressed against the cold in dark coloured jackets and scruffy trousers were yelling and laughing as they attempted to pelt the dog, her heavy body making it difficult to gain the speed needed from a lying start to outrun the onslaught. Another sharp-angled rock connected with her midriff, almost causing her to lose her footing.

The soldier found himself mentally urging the dog to run faster. Falling now would be unthinkable. For a second he thought about how easy it would be to fire a warning shot in the direction of her attackers. 'That would stop 'em,' he thought to himself, but his gloved trigger finger remained rigidly stretched across the trigger guard: he knew it was nothing more than wishful thinking. The military command would not appreciate his sentiment. His personal opinion – that some on this earth deserved to be shot for their cruelty to animals – was most definitely not allowed under the rules of engagement he had to follow.

There was nothing he could do. Helpless, the soldier could only watch as the mutt with the golden-yellow ears attempted to make its escape.

As the injured and obviously very frightened dog increased its speed, the gap between it and the running children finally meant the rocks were falling short as the kids struggled to continue the chase and throw rocks at the same time.

The soldier shook his head in frustration. He had not really thought too much about why the local dogs were treated like this, although it was not the first time he had witnessed it. He knew that his role in Kandahar was just part of the larger war machine that had a huge task ahead to maintain security and render the Taliban ineffective, and he tried not to dwell on the plight of the local dog population for too long.

Right then, the focus of his concentration was in defending his arcs and covering the approach to the airfield along the main road.

To find the source of such seemingly unfounded cruelty, that would horrify dog lovers around the world, the soldier needed to remind himself of the turmoil that Afghanistan had been through in the last forty years. He knew that education – taken as a given for those lucky enough to be born in the West – was a very scarce privilege in Afghanistan: it was either for Afghans with money, who sent their kids to privately funded western schools, or arose from the legacy of coalition intervention which had provided schools for only around half the population who were of schooling age, more so particular in the north of the country. There, the improved security meant that state-run schools were opening their doors and

Afghan teachers no longer felt threatened by acts of retribution from the Taliban.

As a result of Afghanistan's recent history, it was not unusual to find at least two generations of uneducated adults in any family, especially in more rural communities, where Taliban influence made sure schooling was forbidden or threatened; even to the extent that signing for the end-of-month salary involved only an ink pad and a thumb. Education was, then, the sole preserve of the local *mullah* during Friday prayers.

A father can decide what is important and what should be handed down to his sons – everything else is just forgotten, if it was even known in the first place. And animal welfare education was most definitely not a priority in those parts of Afghanistan. Sadly, for a dog in Afghanistan, its losing streak started from the day it was born. Not only was their normally short life one continuous scavenge for the next meal, they had to contend with rabies, a viral disease rife in that part of the world: one that attacks the brain and is, without exception, fatal once the symptoms show themselves. To cap it all, it is predominantly transmitted to humans via the extremely painful method of a dog bite.

Thus the dog, as a species, didn't rate too highly in any popularity stakes. For Afghans, where the opportunities of having their children immunised against measles was rare, so too the chances of finding a hospital that carried the rabies vaccinations, particularly within the vital 24-hour window of being bitten – to give even a remote chance of the vaccination being effective – were next to zero. And then they would need the funds to pay for it, anyway.

Taking it all together, it made most Afghans suitably wary of dogs, and throwing stones to ward them off was their only perceived protection to avoid being bitten. However, those teens had clearly taken it a step further and attempted to deliberately injure the dog rather than just trying to protect themselves.

The fleeing stray disappeared from the soldier's view as it skirted behind a parked Corolla, its front windscreen cracked from top to bottom, green string holding the roof-rack in place. The soldier noted that the dog's right hind flank was stained red from the impact of one of the hurled rocks. Then the soldier's eyes widened as he watched the dog emerge from behind the car and dart hastily towards the sentry position. It was a distance of 100 metres or more but, without turning, panting heavily as it stormed up the slight incline, the dog scooted unerringly into the checkpoint.

The chasing pack of out-of-breath boys that had begun to once more close in on the dog suddenly, en masse, ceased their pursuit as they realised where the dog had chosen to seek refuge.

And so began Lady's residency at entry checkpoint five.

chapter 5

Residency

If anybody happened to have been tasked to head out to the entry checkpoint that day just after the stray dog had found shelter there, they would have been bemused to witness two of the hardened American soldiers, a corporal and one of his team who manned the sentry positions, crouching down by a dog. Their weapons were placed ready by their sides as the trembling dog devoured food from a torn-open brown meal pouch from a military ration pack. The dog was ravenous.

'Who are you?' The young soldier had asked as he crouched down, offering a hand for the nervous dog to sniff, to show he was not a threat.

The tired-looking corporal, his dirt-stained badge of rank clearly visible on the front epaulet of his dusty combat jacket – his combat clothing and ammunition-stuffed webbing was also covered in a fine layer of dust that always covered everything out there – was already crouched down cleaning the wound on the side of the dog with an antiseptic wet-wipe from his combat first-aid kit.

'A stray that ran into the checkpoint. Being chased by a

group of kids' – he indicated the wound – 'throwing rocks at her, little bastards.' He went back to concentrating on cleaning the wound. 'She seems OK – well fed, anyway, judging by the size of her.'

The dog didn't seem to be bothered at all by what he was doing. Her attention was held by the opening of a main meal pouch – this one stew and dumplings, as identified by the printed description on the side of the now discarded packaging.

'Hurt pretty bad,' he added, shaking his head as he dabbed the area where one of the many rocks had punctured the skin.

The dog licked the yound soldier's hand before tucking in again to the offered food pouch. 'I'd say she was pregnant,' he said, as he carefully felt the female dog's obvious belly. 'And not long to go either, I would guess,' he stated, more for the benefit of the corporal than the hungry dog.

'She's *what*?' The corporal looked stunned as he stared at his fellow soldier who was still holding the meal pouch open for the dog to gobble up the contents, not even stopping to breathe as she wolfed down the food on offer.

'You've gotta be kidding!' the corporal cleaning the worst of the injuries said, as he stopped what he was doing to fully digest what had just been announced. 'So that's why she's so fat.' He sighed. 'Like we need a pregnant dog around here . . .' the soldier glanced across at his buddy feeding the dog. 'Command will have a field day,' he exclaimed.

In the armed forces, a soldier's life is controlled from the day he or she walks through the training base doors by an exacting chain of command and a strict military code of conduct that has to be adhered to, no questions asked. To the casual civilian observer, these can look anything from draconian to downright bizarre. The practice of remaining seated at a regimental dinner, for example, banned from leaving the table even for a desperately needed comfort break until the regimental sergeant major calls one, has in the course of military history caught many a fine military man making use of empty wine bottles, their previous contents having caused the problem in the first place. (Thankfully, times have moved on and common sense has prevailed – a charity box now rattles with profit from any early forced trips away from the dinner table.) But certain rules, as all soldiers knew, were in place for important tactical reasons: they saved lives, they maintained the health and welfare of combat troops, they maintained the required discipline to get the job done. And the 'No feral dog rule' was one such general order that had frustrated troops and civilians alike. But it was there for a very serious reason: rabies.

Nearly all the coalition troops serving in Afghanistan were vaccinated against a variety of potential diseases to be found lurking on the battlefield: hepatitis, tetanus and typhoid were just many of the common reasons that troops found themselves in a long line outside their base's medical centre before a deployment. The walk back to the accommodation block would see scores of soldiers rubbing the now sore spot in the middle of their right butt-cheek – a souvenir from the over-zealous medical orderly's delight in stabbing them repeatedly with various vaccine syringes.

But, like Afghans, no soldiers were vaccinated against rabies.

The theory behind it was pretty straightforward, if any of the soldiers cared to think about it: why waste millions on vaccinating troops against a disease that desk-bound analysts and budget-holders had risk-assessed would not be an issue?

The simple solution was to order the soldiers not to interact with the feral animals in the first place and, hey presto, problem solved!

The troops operating from entry checkpoint five that day probably hadn't seen the recent news from the US. Keeping up with family updates was hard enough at times, so the rest of the world's news often had to wait. And whether they would have done anything differently is hard to say.

Just before Lady had stormed into the checkpoint due to being pelted with rocks, the US military had found out that the general order had prevented a soldier from coming forward to report that he had, in fact, been bitten.

Caring for a petite pup on his remote forward operating base in the Afghan mountains, the 24-year-old, on his first tour of duty to the battle-weary country, had known he could risk court martial for disobeying a direct order. But the young soldier had deemed the pup's need greater and, with no officer from senior command paying attention to his activities during downtime, the soldier had started to watch over the lovable stray. Like most soldiers who formed a bond with a dog or cat on the front lines in Afghanistan, the animal had given the soldier brief moments of sanity in an otherwise surreal world of mostly incomprehensible happenings.

But, whether the hapless pup had meant to or not, it bit the naive soldier and had drawn blood. The soldier had tended to the wound himself and, of course, continued caring for the pup. He had chosen to risk not visiting the medical centre, maybe so as to avoid alerting the authorities, assuming that he would be punished and his companion buddy, who now meant the world to him, would be found and destroyed.

It was not until he could no longer hide the fact that he was desperately ill that he had made the decision to take himself to the unit medical facility. But by then it had been too late.

Post-vaccinations cannot combat the aggressive onset of the disease. A hastily arranged medical evacuation flight had transported the dying soldier homeward to Fort Drum, back in the United States, where no amount of intensive care could save him. He had died surrounded by his family, the first US serviceman serving on operations to die of rabies since 1974. A tragic end to kind acts that had brought a small relief to the soldier's otherwise hard-core existence.

'She looks healthy enough,' the corporal judged, as he finished cleaning up the used wet-wipes. 'Nobody important from HQ ever bothers with us here, anyway,' he stated, as if trying to justify what they were about to do.

Which was mostly true. As long as the job was done, then they didn't often receive high-ranking visitors to their diminutive slice of America.

'Welcome to entry checkpoint five,' the soldier said in his Texas drawl, grinning, to the unfazed mum to be, who was still slurping from the ration pack.

And so, the very heavily pregnant bitch gained herself a name for the first time ever: Lady. But, more importantly than that, she also gained a family.

The yound soldier's assessment of Lady's condition was spot on: within days of taking up residency within entry checkpoint five, she gave birth.

Snuggled away under the safety umbrella of the soldiers

guarding the perimeter, she became a proud mum to ten adorable pups. Her highly developed, protective motherly instincts took over and not only did the tan and white former feral carry out her motherly duties with zeal, she also cared fiercely for the coalition troops who had sheltered her at her moment of most need.

The soldiers assumed that Lady was returning the favour, considering the soldiers as part of her extended family. From a security perspective, as far as the troops were concerned, Lady added another level of security to their vulnerable position. When unwanted Afghan nationals approached the checkpoint, Lady would charge out across the open no-man's-land barking like a dog possessed, warning all that this was now her territory. The approaching locals would stop immediately, terrified by the sight of the snarling dog. Hackles raised and spittle flying from her mouth, Lady dominated the ground between them with terrifying ease.

The soldiers were more than happy to have an early warning system of the four-legged kind in place; in fact, more times than they cared to note, Lady got wind of approaching visitors to the checkpoint long before the dedicated sentries ever did. Watching her ears prick upright, searching for a signal from outer space, they knew she could hear even the faintest sound of somebody nearing the checkpoint. And, as if on cue, she would launch from her resting spot fearlessly towards the source of the intrusion.

Danielle who had been across to the checkpoint to assist with ensuring the soldiers were looking after Lady as best they could, was also amazed by Lady's ability to stand down immediately, once she realised that the approaching strangers to the checkpoint were coalition troops. Her threatening and very aggressive 'on-guard' stance – her hackles raised along the back of her tan neck – would immediately relax into the gentle, affectionate mum that had first arrived many weeks before.

The soldiers who sauntered over to see the pups tried desperately to maintain the macho, rugged image of a soldier but would melt instantly the moment they held one of Lady's tiny new-borns. To know they that had saved these pups and their mum from a desperate fate outside the wire gave them a sense of pride that their mundane and isolated day-to-day job didn't.

Most of the visiting soldiers or contractors would stop by to see her wriggling litter, gently lifting a clingy pup from the tangled mass of paws and tiny ears as each one struggled to stay tightly wrapped against its brothers and sisters. Lady would sit patiently on her haunches, just to one side, carefully surveying the proceedings.

But for the locals Afghans outside the wire, those who still felt grieved that the westerners had invaded their lands and those who demonstrated a misplaced sense of loyalty to the Taliban by directing their collective anger toward the coalition troops, then the checkpoint's new, four-legged security guard was an easy target for their displeasure.

Many times, Danielle was called over the radio to the checkpoint to suture a nasty-looking wound Lady had received from a thrown rock as she resolutely defended her new home, and Danielle and the lads began to seriously fear for the safety of their guardian dog. Except for tying her to an immovable object somewhere in the compound 24 hours a day, there was not a lot the soldiers could think to do except be at the ready to patch her up if and when required.

And, as word spread of their companion buddy and her brood at the checkpoint, the minority of Afghan nationals still sharing an affinity for the departed Taliban regime were not the only ones displeased with Lady's residency at the entry checkpoint. The general order banning all contact with dogs was still in force and, by all official accounts, Lady and her pups were only adorable to one federal police officer and the soldiers at the checkpoint.

Kandahar airfield superiors soon heard of the antics of the protective former stray at entry checkpoint five and, without care for the circumstances surrounding the situation, a destruction order was swiftly issued and passed down the chain of command ordering the early demise of Lady and her pups.

Summoned to see her superior officer, Danielle had been handed the brief but all too meaningful order, printed on a piece of A4 paper.

'How could they?' Danielle exclaimed as she read the issued order one more time.

It was a senseless waste of life. It was no use trying to explain it to the higher authorities – they just wouldn't understand, having never been hidden away behind a sandbag at the checkpoint as bullets tore into the hessian material just inches from your head, holding on to Lady for comfort and reassurance in those moments of madness.

Lady was one of those manning the checkpoint. She had stood with them side by side as the soldiers faced the enemy. After all that she had been through to survive, showing nothing but gratitude to her western companions, she was destined to die at the hands of the good guys.

Danielle took up the order and asked the officer if that was all.

Without comment, just a nod, she was dismissed.

Back home in Australia, Danielle's home had been at risk of turning into a wildlife refuge before she was sent overseas. And all involved in animal rescue wherever it took place in the world had long ago realised the importance of education in promoting animal welfare. Wondering if education would work here, in Afghanistan, was something to be considered.

There were many soldiers who used the opportunity of the security nets that were thrown around a remote provincial village while the commanders of their patrol attended a *shura* meeting with village elders, to deliver an impromptu English lesson or hygiene clinic. For many of the soldiers with a background in education, it was their way of bringing something tangibly positive to the dangerous time spent on the ground. The soldiers didn't have to go the extra mile but they did, and that opportunity for education was rarely turned away by the Afghan people. The village elders who remembered the prosperous pre-Soviet days of a moderate Afghanistan in the sixties and seventies understood the need for their young to be educated.

Just as Danielle and the soldiers of entry checkpoint five were proving, people often forgot that soldiers were also just people doing a job. Caring for an innocent animal was part of her make-up as a person, just as it was for the soldiers who had first given Lady a safe haven.

Danielle realised she had to go on the offensive if she wanted to do something positive and lasting for Lady and her pups. The Australian police officer, who was already more than extremely busy each day with the task that had brought her to Afghanistan, decided to pile on the pressure, adding animal welfare activist and dog rescuer to her job résumé.

And she, along with the support of other coalition internationals sharing her passion for the feral population, started trying to rehome Lady and her pups.

The 'how' was going to be the extremely hard part.

chapter 6

Growing Up

Socks' daily priority had changed – finding water took on as much importance as food these days.

Dust-devils danced together across the arid ground in tag teams, lifting the discarded food wrappers, empty plastic water bottles and other unwanted human detritus along with them until they died, dumping the reluctant debris back down with all the other rubbish again. The landscape of Afghanistan was resembling a colossal rubbish tip more each day.

The ground was parched and cracked. The winter rains and cold, sleepless nights were a distant memory. Now, the air was thick with fine dust particles that clung to whatever they came in contact with. Socks's sleek body continually wore a coat of dust these days. Everything did. People, houses, cars, even household furniture. Everything. Nothing was immune from the blanket of dust. Socks would rise from the ground and shake himself as if he was drying his rain-soaked coat in the winter months only now, instead, a cloud of dust would waft away from him.

The heat was a draining constant on anything that moved. Living by night was now the norm. Finding a safe, shady area to curl up and sleep was Socks's only concern during the day. Even so, black flies would buzz into his mouth and eyes as he slept: at first an annoyance, snapping and barking to making them stop, but he had long ago realised he wouldn't catch them, and they wouldn't go away.

It took too much effort and it was far too hot with his long, brindled coat to be even remotely energetic in trying to do anything. Panting quickly and heavily to regulate his body temperature, he would try to lie as still as possible, adopting the pose of a million stray dogs the world over during the hottest days of the year.

Socks wouldn't have known it, but the summer-time temperatures in Kandahar could easily reach a body-sapping 45°C. On a cool day. At night, the winds did little to bring the temperature much below 35°, but Socks would have no choice but to embark on his scavenge for food and water.

The old lady who had befriended Socks well over a year ago had known he would change his routine, and she was prepared for his late evening arrivals. After all, she had lived much longer than Socks, witnessing the ceaseless ebb and flow of life on the streets of the only city she had ever known. During the hottest part of the day, at least she could retire to the inviting coolness of her high-ceilinged living room, the battery-operated fan, a present from her husband, making a constant burring noise as it worked tirelessly to keep her cool.

Everybody who lived in Afghanistan knew the street dogs changed their living habits with the changing of the seasons. The nightly soundtrack of barking that echoed off the high compound walls that criss-crossed the city was relentless during the summer months, but it was life in

Afghanistan and nothing could change it. The persistent barking could only stop you from getting a good night's sleep if you let it: most Afghans fell asleep regardless of the noise that drove most unaccustomed westerners mad as they tried to drown it out.

As the early evening settled over Kandahar, the roads would see less and less traffic as men across the city arrived home to take their traditional place at the head of the table, surrounded by their large family, ready for the evening meal that brought them all together.

Socks would take the opportunity of the easing flow of cars to scamper safely across the poorly lit highway. Running along the drainage ditch and crossing the barren expanse of land, he would no longer stop to call for his mum. He knew she was never coming back. Now, the lone survivor was focused solely on making it safely to the food and water the kindly old lady would place out for him.

Strangely, she was often not there to greet him these days. Socks would eagerly search ahead, towards the end of the alley, for his human companion in her long black dress and brightly coloured head scarf, and felt pained when he could not see her. But, as if to console him, there was always the bowl of long grained rice, mixed as always with tiny pieces of gristly meat, placed by the rear wheel-arch of the abandoned car. A slightly rusting metal bucket of freshly topped up water was always there too, for Socks to drink from.

When the old lady did reappear, old age seemed to have suddenly caught up with her: she struggled to lower herself into a crouching position to reach her canine companion these days, and she coughed and spluttered into a tissue as she rubbed him with her free hand. But Socks did not really notice. He was transfixed by the undivided attention she gave him. She always made the effort – no matter how much pain her failing body gave her – to fuss over her animal companion, and her eyes would light up when she saw the playful young dog approaching, his tail wagging furiously behind him as he trotted up the alley to greet her.

Socks would lick her hand as she playfully ruffled his hair and stroked his long, floppy ears before, together, they went through the rituals of the routine they had followed since day one.

Always the old lady would hold back some food for the young dog in her right hand, waiting for him to lick every last grain of rice from the bowl before teasing him to sit as she opened her palm to reveal the last morsel of meat.

When he had gently taken the final treat from her, he would roll onto his back against the bullet-hard ground, encouraging the old lady to rub his belly.

Both of them were content. The rest of the world could have ended in those moments and neither would have cared. At the end of the secluded alley, hidden away from prying eyes, they both enjoyed being in each other's company and both were sad every time their time together had to come to an end.

But Socks was a growing dog and, over the summer and into the autumn and approaching winter months, the food the old lady left him was not enough to sustain him. He would scavenge throughout the night, searching to satisfy the hunger and thirst pains that came in the early hours of the morning. But Socks had to be careful. There were many feral dogs that lived in the surrounding areas of Kandahar, and all claimed different sections of the streets as their own.

Feral dogs are extremely territorial and can be very pack-orientated. Roaming as a group, they can be fearsomely aggressive if provoked or challenged.

Socks would stop now and again to sniff through the discarded family rubbish dumped unceremoniously outside every high-walled family compound, the brightly painted metal gates the only weakness in the sun-hardened walls that guarded the houses inside. Pawing the rotting rubbish would normally reveal a snack or two. Beggars were most definitely not choosers. But Socks knew that if he strayed into the wrong street and was cornered by a pack then there would be little chance of survival. His only hope would be that he could outrun them, but his short legs were no match for the taller-standing mongrels that roamed those streets. If just one managed to catch onto his rear legs . . .

Most packs were led by an alpha male dog, who demonstrated his right to be pack leader with displays of overwhelming aggression towards whichever young male was unwise enough to challenge him. He would dominate his pack with teeth and aggression. Together, the males were fiercely protective of their females and as an attacking pack they were a force to be reckoned with.

Socks carefully sniffed the lower sections of the compound walls that lined the darkened alleys and the normally broken lamp-posts for the telltale smell of another dog's territory. If he caught the pungent aroma of a male dog's mark then he would immediately scoot off, trotting off to the presumed safety of the next alley, senses on full alert for any indication that he might be in trouble.

The happy-go-lucky youngster had learnt the hard way that a hungry pack did not welcome strangers into its midst,

especially ones bidding for a share of the sparse food offerings. Territory with a supply of food to call home was hard to
come by on the unwelcoming streets of Afghanistan.

Socks had once wandered into what had looked like a
fairly quiet street, sniffing furiously for warning scents but
finding none. A white Corolla pickup truck, once the vehicle
of choice of the Taliban, had cruised slowly along the pitted
mud road, a cloud of dust following closely behind until the
wheels ran onto some dampened road, kept wet by a proud
shop keeper eager to keep his wares dust-free.

Bearded shop keepers sat in chairs outside the darkened
interiors of their shops under the shade of brightly coloured
shop awnings, waiting to greet whoever might be their next
customer.

Socks trotted casually past the first of the shops, which
was selling housewares – bowls and saucepans, before the
sudden hammering of metal scared him into a mini-sprint as
he passed in front of an open cargo container doubling as a
shop. Somewhere deep inside, a man was busy fitting together
intricately detailed metal wood-burners.

When Socks realised there was nothing to fear, he eased
back into a casual trot as he continued to move along the
street. The very few Afghans walking along towards him
ignored what was to them just another street dog.

As his sensitive canine nostrils picked up the appealing
scent of raw meat, he quickened his pace. Up ahead, hanging by their back hooves outside a butcher's shop, were two
decapitated goats swaying gently in the afternoon heat.
Flies had been quick to buzz around the recently skinned
animals. His excitement overwhelmed his senses and he
didn't see the two ragged-looking mongrels lying in the
gutter, their bodies a fluffy mismatch of winter coat hair that

was still to shed and the new, thinner summer coat trying to push through.

They may have looked like they were sleeping, curled up head-to-toe in the dust, but being strays they would always sleep with one eye open, ready for the slightest hint of danger coming their way. They sensed Socks at the same time and both launched into the attack as one.

Socks had yet to learn that nearly every butcher in Afghanistan would tolerate a few chosen ferals hanging around near to the shop. It was their insurance against their shop being besieged by hungry dogs each day, as the privileged dogs provided the muscle to ward off any other unwelcome dog visitors to the premises. In return, the unregulated 'doormen' would be fed the leftover scraps from the blood-stained floor, the unwritten rule of never crossing the threshold into the shop somehow communicated by human to dog.

Luckily, the smell of the hanging meat was pretty overpowering, even from a distance, so Socks was still some way from the shop door when he saw the blurred shapes coming for him. He turned tail instantly, his rear legs driving him forward as he sprinted hard to escape. The chase was thankfully short-lived as the butcher's shop dogs were loath to pursue the intruder too far – they never left the vicinity of their shop for long for fear another dog would seize the opportunity to take up residency. But they had given Socks a clear message: Don't come back.

Just like the thousands of other stray dogs destined to roam until they died, life was a rollercoaster of mini successes and failures: successes were finding food and water and a safe place to sleep each night; failures were going hungry or suffering injuries at the hands of humans, other dogs or vehicles.

Socks, as far as ferals went, had actually been very lucky so far. At nearly a year and half old, he had managed to lead a pretty charmed life. But, as he was about to drastically find out, lucky streaks always came to an abrupt end at some point.

chapter 7

Aseel

The old man stumbled along the side of the dusty road, still wearing the same white *salwar kameez* trousers and the dark, grubby suit jacket that he had been wearing the day before, when they had met the coalition soldier on the barren track to the south of his village.

Of course, at that meeting he had been surrounded by the other village elders who had come along to support him. And his good friend, the school teacher, had been on hand to offer to translate the foreign tongue for them all.

But today he was alone. No one else had been able to travel with him.

The rickety bus had taken countless hours to travel the long, uncomfortable road to reach Kandahar. It had not been a pleasant journey: with the bus crammed full of his fellow countrymen, who were all attempting to scratch a living in the midst of war, it had been extremely claustrophobic, while the stop-start nature of the bus ride had, at one point, caused him to curse the driver out loud. Thankfully, no one had heard him over the noise of the badly serviced engine and the child next to him crying constantly.

He hoped his long journey had not been in vain, as he hoped to take word of his son's condition back to their family. Or, better still, he would find his son fit and healthy and able to travel back with him. His son was responsible for tending the family crops, and he needed him back at work.

More than once he had cursed the day that the Taliban had decided to use his peaceful village as a staging post for an attack against the foreign troops. He didn't care for the Taliban in the slightest – as a poppy farmer, they had caused him nothing but trouble when they were in power as, just like that, they had banned the poppy trade altogether. But now that they realised it could, in part, fund their war against the Americans, the poppy production had increased threefold.

The old man didn't care much for politics. Just like everybody else, he only wanted to make a decent living to support his family. And he was fed up with everybody telling him how he should do it.

Once the hellish journey was over and he was standing back on firm ground in the middle of Kandahar, he had struggled to get his bearings. It had been a long time since he had last visited Afghanistan's second largest city, and everything had changed a great deal. For one thing, there had been a surge in building work, rendering his memory map of the journey out towards the airport useless. But he could ponder 'progress' another day. He was there for one reason only.

Many times he had to ask the local roadside vendors, all sitting patiently by the side of their cluttered, overstocked stalls waiting for their next paying customer, if he was walking in the right direction to reach the home of the Americans at the military airbase. He had never been taught to read, so the metal road signs placed at regular intervals along the edge of the busy highway were meaningless gobbledegook: just big white letters on a blue background.

The cars raced by the old man far too close for his comfort: he was sure they had no thought for his safety. In fact, twice he even thought he had been hit as the *vroom* and rush of air from a speeding vehicle had buffeted him savagely, before he was covered in a cloud of dust. But he carried little in the way of money as it was, so he really couldn't afford the luxury of a taxi. The bus to Kandahar has been more expensive that he had anticipated, and if he was to have any money for the return journey back to his village then he needed to conserve funds, especially if, as he hoped, his son would be with him.

The further he walked along the Afghan highway, the more the chill Afghan winter wind went straight through him, his suit jacket no match for the cold. And nor was he used to walking these distances any more. In fact, he was feeling decidedly tired. Surely, by now, he should be getting close to the airfield?

His eyesight was poor and, scanning the dust-laden distance, he could see no indication of the airport complex. Finally, the old man stopped. Pulling his scarf tightly around his neck, he resigned himself to the fact that he doubted he could walk much farther. He hunched over dejectedly as he debated what course of action he should take next.

Aseel was in a hurry.

He had been tasked by his uncle to pick up and deliver a quantity of the plastic drainage pipes that his uncle's company manufactured; the pipes were required for a new construction job starting the next day, and Aseel was already running late. Normally, he would have taken a very reliable but slow bus to get to his uncle's warehouse, but he had jumped into the first battered yellow Corolla taxi that was available. Speaking in his rapid Pashtun, he had directed the elderly driver out past the airport and towards the industrial estate and the warehouse that held their supplies.

Aseel knew it was too far to walk even for a fit young guy like himself, especially on a bitterly cold day.

In his early twenties, Aseel was a stocky young man, aware of his appearance and mindful of keeping his moustache neatly trimmed. Pipe manufacturing was not his first choice as a career, but circumstances had dictated that his first choice was not available to him, and so he worked for his uncle and that was that.

In a country where employment was rife amongst the young male population, he knew of no Afghan who would turn down the opportunity for an honest day's labour.

He was grateful that he had a steady job. Many others did not. Besides, his father would have demanded that he worked hard. His father had been a good Muslim and, whilst stern and to the point, and not suffering fools gladly, he had instilled in his son a strong commitment to help others and always to lead by example: he would have opened his door to any soul in need. He had also brought up his son to take nothing for granted and to respect his elders. Aseel was not going to let the memory of his father down, so when his uncle had offered him work after his father's death, he had thanked him and accepted the generous offer.

Aseel looked out at the passing landscape, the yellowish mud compound walls that flashed by were interspersed with rubbish-filled alleys and mostly Afghan men going about their everyday lives. It was the everyday picture of life that Aseel had only really ever known.

Turning to look several hundred yards ahead through the dusty windscreen of the taxi, Aseel noticed an old man crouching at the side of the road. Even from this distance, Aseel realised the old man's clothing was clearly not suitable for the bitter, late-afternoon chill.

The aged Afghan looked in distress and, without a second thought, Aseel ordered the driver to pull to a stop next to the shivering old man.

Pushing the passenger door open, Aseel greeted the old man: 'Peace be upon you,' instantly feeling the cold air rush in to replace the inviting warmth from the car's one heater. 'Please come inside and share my taxi,' he added.

The old man stared intently at Aseel for a few seconds, clearly weighing up the reasons for the young man's generosity before cracking a smile, the gap where his missing two front teeth used to be clearly visible. He hobbled over to the waiting car and struggled to bend his body into the back of the vehicle and the respite from the cold it offered.

Pleasantries exchanged, Aseel enquired as to where the old man wanted to go. As the taxi pulled away from the kerb, the old man rapidly began to explain his story – of the day the foreign troops had attacked the Taliban position in his village.

His voice dropped to a murmur as he recalled how his eldest son had been seriously injured in the subsequent battle. Then, beginning to wave his arms around as he warmed to his story, he portrayed the big black American helicopter that had landed and the soldiers who had run from the helicopter to whisk his injured son away. He had not been allowed to go with them: the soldiers already at the scene before the helicopter had arrived had held him back as the flying machine had lifted into the clear afternoon sky.

He lowered his head and, with his voice almost at a whisper, he explained his pain at not understanding where the foreigners had taken his child. He had waited many hours until a chance meeting with a British soldier on a track that had eventually led to him taking on the tiring, long journey to Kandahar.

Aseel listened intently, now and again struggling to understand the old man's dialect – just because they were both from the south did not mean they both spoke the same Pashto – but gaining the gist of the sorrowful tale and nodding thoughtfully as he acknowledged the predicament the old man found himself in.

Thinking it through quickly, Aseel reassured the old man not to worry. As Aseel spoke some English and the old man clearly didn't speak any at all, he promised he would accompany him to the gates of Kandahar airfield.

Looking somewhat relieved, the old man settled back into the seat of the taxi as they drove towards the airfield, both men lost in their own thoughts.

With what warmth there was from the late afternoon sun disappearing quickly as it started its slow decline behind the darkened, jagged mountains to the west, the taxi pulled up well short of entry checkpoint five. Only vehicles with official business at the airfield were allowed to travel further.

Aseel handed the driver tattered Afghani notes for the both of them as he and the old man left the cosiness of the vehicle behind them. The afternoon wind had picked up considerably now that they were well outside the over-populated areas of Kandahar. With fewer buildings as obstacles to check the gusts' progress, mini dust-devils swirled and danced across the open ground surrounding the checkpoint as Aseel and the old man approached carefully.

Aseel was a staunch supporter of the coalition's intervention in Afghanistan. He hated the Taliban. He had good reason to. But he was also very aware that he was clearly Afghan and that one wrong move on his part as he walked up to the checkpoint could lead to him being shot – albeit mistakenly but still, he would have been shot.

He knew the coalition troops had suffered terrible casualties at the hands of his so-called fellow countrymen, and so the soldiers guarding this checkpoint would rightly be wary of him.

He indicated for the old man to stand fast as he approached the sentry post to explain why they were there. Oddly to him, Aseel thought he could hear barking in the distance and the sounds of people laughing, but he ignored what he thought he had heard and held up his arms, demonstrating that he carried no weapons and was not a threat. Carefully forming his words using his very basic English, Aseel attempted to explain the reason for their visit to the checkpoint.

The soldiers, whilst employing all the security protocols they had been trained to implement, realised that Aseel and the old man were of little threat. Besides, they had dealt with situations like this many times before, and the senior corporal immediately understood what Aseel was trying to explain.

Giving Aseel a quick body search and confirming that all he carried was a battered mobile phone, the corporal indicated for him to move to the side of the checkpoint: 'You can wait there for the old man to return.'

Aseel had only planned on helping the old man to find the airfield and had not intended on staying, but he didn't know how to phrase: 'But I am not staying,' in English. Before he knew it, the soldier had searched the old man and was escorting him through the entrance to the checkpoint.

Aseel looked up at the fortified checkpoint, the RPG-resistant, high walls topped with razor wire, deterrent enough for the casual attacker but little protection against the 107mm rockets that he knew were used now and again to target most of the military bases in Afghanistan.

It was a well-known fact that to be around coalition troops courted trouble: the Taliban did not differentiate between Muslim and non-Muslim when they started an attack. Aseel took a quick look around, but realised he had no idea what he should look for to indicate an attack was coming.

And he was thirsty. It had been a while since he had last drunk any water. Constantly breathing in the dry, arid dust that was swirling around him was making his throat sore.

Once again, the sounds of a barking dog, not like it was being aggressive but as if it was playing along with the over-excited voices of foreigners shouting happily, gradually drifted across on the wind, becoming louder as Aseel listened. As the sounds became clearer, he realised that it was actually a woman's voice he could hear. Curiosity gained the upper hand and Aseel moved towards the corner of the sandbagged wall, completely forgetting he had been told to stay and wait for the old man to return.

As he peered around the corner, his eyes lit up.

There in front of him, walking towards the main gate, were what he guessed to be two American soldiers: the man wearing his drab camouflage uniform that all American soldiers wore, his rifle hanging by its sling down his side; the woman, with brunette hair pulled back into a ponytail, wearing light brown overalls. But what drew his attentions was the largish, golden-coloured dog with big floppy ears that was jumping around between the two of them as she clapped her hands to encourage the dog more. The man just grinned at the two of them as they all walked along together.

Neither had noticed Aseel, and the woman started doing a sort of dance with the dog as it jumped up and around her fast-moving legs. Both were clearly enjoying themselves and oblivious to everything else around them.

Without a second thought for the protocols to be adopted on a military base, Aseel moved towards the two soldiers.

'Woah, stop there!' a voice boomed across to him. 'That's close enough.' To his dismay, Aseel now saw that the male soldier had adopted a defensive stance as he faced him, his left arm out straight and his right hand flexed on the pistol grip of the rifle.

The interaction with the dog had ceased and, to Aseel's distress, the dog had adopted an 'on-guard' stance as well.

He needed to act quickly. Without hesitation, Aseel stopped short and held out his hands to show he had nothing concealed and meant no harm, mentally chiding himself for forgetting the universal gesture required when approaching American soldiers.

'I am Aseel. I am a veterinarian,' he exclaimed. 'You play with d-dog. I l-like dog,' he stammered in his broken English, as he looked to the dog as if for moral support.

The woman looked Aseel up and down curiously. When she spoke directly to him, it was in an accent that Aseel had never heard before. It sounded odd even for an American.

'You are a veterinarian?' she asked, as if not believing what he had said.

'Yes.' Aseel responded honestly to the woman. 'I am Aseel, veterinarian of animals,' he stated, to ensure they both understood.

The woman approached him. 'Who trained you, Aseel, veterinarian of animals?' she asked.

Aseel immediately picked up the doubt that was carried in her voice. 'Americans train me as para-vet,' Aseel quickly explained, in the best English he could muster.

The woman nodded as if satisfied. She had obviously heard of the Americans training vets, Aseel realised.

'I am Danielle. It's good to meet you, Aseel.' The woman held out her right hand as she smiled directly at him.

Aseel had never shaken a woman's hand before and wasn't really sure if he was meant to, but he went with it and did anyway.

As he did so, the dog's aggressive stance melted instantly and it trotted over to sniff his trouser leg. Once satisfied he was OK, it strolled back to sit by Danielle's leg. 'And this is Lady,' she added, ruffling the top of Lady's golden head.

Aseel recognised easily that 'Lady' had just given birth. Her nipples looked swollen and sore from feeding what he correctly guessed was obviously a largish litter.

Without introducing the male soldier, Danielle's eyes widened with excitement as an idea seemed to form in her mind. 'Have you taken part in animal surgeries?' she enquired. She was completely focused on Aseel, waiting for his answer.

'Of course,' Aseel responded proudly, as if there should never have been any doubt.

Without actually explaining what it was she wanted from him, Danielle smiled broadly and simply said, 'Then I need your help, please.'

Aseel was shocked that an American should ask him for help. He was actually quite confused – the Americans had everything, everybody knew that. So why would they need his help?

'I will help you, but first I need some water. I am thirsty,' he said, assuming they were going to ask him to carry or lift something. He needed water before he did anything physical. He hadn't realised that Danielle did not mean she needed his help right that second.

Her plans for him went much longer-term than that.

'Water?' Danielle asked in reply. 'That's no problem!' She once more patted the dog's head as it proudly sat by her side.

Aseel smiled. But continued to look very confused.

chapter 8

The Clinic

The earlier chill of the Afghan night had all but been forgotten. The morning sun was making its steady rise across a clear blue sky, bringing the temperature up to double digits. Taliban incoming mortar fire had taken care of any chance of sleep during the night. Luckily, nobody at the checkpoint had been injured but protocols had meant that all hands had been required to be awake and at their 'stand to' position long after the last incoming mortar had been fired.

Danielle knew she had to do everything she could to make sure the innocent little pups survived. Losing them was not an option. And she hoped that her plan to help the puppies would be effective against any of the senior chain of command's destruction orders.

Danielle had begun to deliver animal welfare lessons and health clinics. Not only this, but she had gone into overdrive to rehome every single one of Lady's pups. But Danielle well understood that it was not just a case of asking folk stationed at Kandahar airfield if they wanted a cute little pup to take home. There was a lot more to it than that. Danielle formed a team of like-minded volunteers from within the ranks at the base, who turned their hands to organising fundraising activities to help secure the required amount for each pup's welfare and transport. This also involved designing posters and advertising that explained each bundle of craziness's – as Danielle often referred to the now playful and inquisitive puppies – character, to help lure in potential new owners.

In her team, and keen to do something positive for the feral dogs, was an American military vet deployed to Afghanistan and tasked to look after the many working dogs that operated alongside the western troops on the ground by sniffing out roadside bombs and weapons caches – a tireless and very dangerous job. She also had an Australian doctor on the team, along with soldiers who just wanted to do their bit to make a difference.

However, Danielle's hastily assembled volunteers immediately encountered a major stumbling block.

Even with her Aussie determination and enthusiasm, which the senior military command found almost impossible to refuse, Danielle desperately needed good-quality vaccines for each dog, including a rabies vaccine, at the very least. The military had not signed up to deliver vaccinations to mere strays, and they were loath to release any of the imported vaccines for the working dogs population for Danielle's clinic to use.

Her only option was to import them from the United States to ensure she could continue to carry out her plan of setting up a veterinary clinic just outside the main entrance to Kandahar airfield. And so Danielle herself paid for the vaccinations for each and every one of the pups that needed to be rehomed, and knew that she would have to pay for the potential patients she hoped to receive at the clinic.

Aseel had already proved to be worth his weight in gold. He was genuinely determined to be involved in animal health. Danielle was amazed at his enthusiasm, compared to the reluctance and low motivation overall of the majority of her Afghan Police recruits. And having an Afghan who could translate in an area that he actually believed in was a double bonus.

There was no doubt of his hatred for the Taliban. They had killed Aseel's father for promoting Aseel's education and his use of western medicines.

Aseel had been a teenager when his father was taken away and executed.

Danielle had listened quietly as he had told his tale. Restrained by cultural differences, there was little else she could do.

Instead of descending into a world of revenge and violence, Aseel had followed the wise words of his father and continued his education. His love of animals had mapped out his chosen career path and his ambition had been to open his own animal clinic in Kandahar. Due to lack of opportunities to join the government veterinary training programme, he had started teaching himself veterinary techniques.

Danielle learned that there was an actual functioning organisation responsible for the vets who had been trained and were now working in Afghanistan. Unbeknown to many, the Afghan Veterinary Association, based out of a headquarters in Kabul, attempted to promote best practice amongst its members where it could. Sadly, they had been unable to offer Aseel a place on any long-term training programme.

He had not been deterred, however, and, seeking the support of the United States Agency for International Development Programme, which among many other reconstruction and rejuvenation projects provided training for remote village vets, he had learnt the basic skills to become a *para-vet*, technically an assistant to a formally qualified veterinarian, allowing Aseel to treat the lifeblood of any village life: their cattle. To say he was a fast learner was an understatement. To hone the basic skills he had been taught, he had worked for nearly two years at a rural vet clinic in Farah Province, well away from the reach of the Taliban responsible for his father's fate.

Returning to Kandahar to find the Taliban still very much controlling everyday life, and with informants everywhere, he had had no choice but to stay off the radar and not become involved in any type of veterinary employ, lest his name be recognised. His uncle had then very bravely stepped in to offer him work in the family business, confirming to Aseel that he was doing the right thing for the time being.

Aseel was now able to practise his veterinary skills under the protective umbrella of the troops at entry checkpoint five, whenever Danielle sent him a text saying he was needed. It was an arrangement that worked well both ways. But Danielle had not anticipated that Aseel would pester her for homework to hone his knowledge. Without fail, every morning, he would present his answers for marking, and his passion for animal welfare was infectious to any of the coalition team that worked alongside him.

The fact that Aseel had even secured extra work as a taxi driver so that he could afford to buy medicines that might be needed at the animal clinic was a sign of real hope for Afghanistan. It was extraordinary, particularly considering that he was risking severe reprisals from the Taliban operating in and around Kandahar if they were to discover his support of the troops at the airfield.

Lady, placid and docile when in the company of friends,

became the ideal model for Danielle to demonstrate to Aseel anatomy or practical suturing skills – the latter thanks to the dog's unnerving ability always to be found in the thick of it with the angry locals. In fact, as Lady was so willing to be used to demonstrate animal-welfare techniques, and knowing full well that none of the western working dogs would be released for such a task, Danielle decided to use Lady for the demos during the clinics.

There was an extensive network of local expatriates living and working in Kandahar: security and construction projects employed the majority of western contractors to be found that far south, but there were also smaller, non-governmental organisations with operations in Kandahar as well. And where you found westerners, you could bet your last shrimp on a barbie on Bondi beach that the dog lovers amongst their staff would have probably adopted an adorable little street pup at some point during their travels.

There were not many animal lovers working in-country that could say no to the Afghan puppy cuteness factor: it was apparent that emotions always assumed that an apparently lonely pup on the dangerous streets of Afghanistan required western intervention to survive. Pretty quickly, though, most would-be rescuers would realise that plucking the pup from the street had been the easy part, and that a whole process was only just beginning.

Ahead there would be some serious obstacles to overcome if the dog was to survive into adulthood. The new, four-legged addition to their protected compound would require, at the very least, a series of vaccinations and treatments essential for the vulnerable little whippersnapper in a country as disease-ridden as Afghanistan. And whilst there were private Afghan veterinary practices dotted across the country, it was very hit and miss as to the level of experience and knowledge that the practice owners actually had, especially relating to dogs. Very often they only specialised – if that word could be used – in providing mostly over-priced and incorrect diagnoses for the village goats, sheep, cows and, of course, the hard-working donkeys.

Then there was the question of the quality of the vet's medical supplies – out-of-date stock was common, while finding any Afghan vet with any quantity of rabies, parvo or distemper vaccines was a toughie. And then the most important consideration: whether it had been stored correctly. Refrigeration protocols were of paramount importance for vaccines and it didn't help that most of Afghanistan suffered from continued electricity blackouts, which were especially prevalent during the hottest summer days.

Sadly but not unexpectedly for Afghanistan, and just like many other organisations with good intentions, the Afghanistan Veterinary Association lacked the resources and funding required to maintain any reasonable level of interaction with the many clinics spread far and wide across the country, leaving the quality of its members' professional conduct sometimes seriously lacking. Put simply, the AVA's ability to effect change for the better was at times questionable.

And so Danielle began to offer vaccinations and general health checks to the pets of the expat community, and there was an instant demand for her team's services. If it could encourage or help anyone to look after a stray from the street, then that was a result.

Word amongst the local Afghan population also spread quickly, about an American woman who spoke in a strange-sounding accent, and who gave open-air animal clinics at the airfield. Afghan nationals from all walks of life, curious to know exactly what Danielle and her team were offering, ventured out to take a look.

Most of the Afghan visitors to the workshops just could not comprehend that Australia was not part of America. After all, the woman giving them spoke English. Danielle gave up trying to explain. It was hard to work out if the onlookers to her clinics were there just because she was a woman who did not cover herself from head to toe in a *burka* and seemed at ease talking out loud to the gathered men, or because she and the team completely doted over what most of the locals perceived as dirty dogs.

What everyone hoped, as it was the reason they had started the clinic, was that maybe the Afghan onlookers really were genuinely interested!

Either way, the soldiers were thrilled that they had the opportunity especially with the position of the base senior command, to try and make a difference, no matter how small, to the lives of the street dogs. They knew that they could but only try. And besides, it gave them something positive to do around the frustrating mentoring of the Afghan police recruits. It also allowed Danielle a platform to continue working to find homes for all of Lady's pups, she had side stepped the destruction orders and was now on a mission.

From the get go, the emphasis of the clinic was to demonstrate that dogs could be a source of companionship rather than just to be used in dog fights, a pastime that was increasingly popular in Afghanistan, or there to be tortured as a warped form of amusement.

It was pure joy to observe the onlookers staring open-mouthed at Danielle, simply due to the fact that she was talking to a dog. And the moment would get even better when Danielle held up her hand and simply said, 'Sit!' There was nobody in the crowd who believed that they had just seen a dog obey a woman speaking in English.

Nor did the clinic team foresee the arrival of hordes of Afghan children, who seemed to really enjoy the open clinic forum, with some of them keen to touch and handle the puppies or even Lady herself. More surprising – and confirmation that the programme was a success – was when the team actually realised that some of the young Afghan children were returning again and again, and would happily chat about what they had learnt during their last visit. Result!

Maybe there really was hope for Afghanistan. Encouraging in expats was one thing, but if the team could actually convince a local dog owner to bring their own dog in for a vaccination, they could attempt to highlight the seriousness of rabies, a disease that seemed completely underrated and simply referred to as 'the crazy dog disease', and that would be an even better result.

And, after a while, bring them in they did. Dogs that were injured or sick would arrive at the clinic for treatment. It was an out and out success, even to the point where Danielle's team started to receive attention from veterinary associations in the United States. Articles, too, began appearing about the clinic, in *National Geographic*, and in the Australian press.

The mission to rehome the pups was also cracking on, too. With a constant flow of visitors, Lady's pups were becoming extremely socialised and with the hard-hitting adoption campaign in place, it wasn't long before the number of pups that had once been overwhelming in the cramped entry checkpoint were now finding homes. Within the space of just a few months, Lady's pups had homes in Canada, America and the Netherlands.

Freighting the pups out of Afghanistan, with all the accompanying administration and paperwork that was required, whilst rewarding, was also extremely exhausting. Danielle was still managing all of this during her own time as her self-appointed mission to be the local dog rescuer obviously could not encroach on her official job responsibilities.

When she finally returned to Australia and took the time to look back on her tour of Afghanistan, everybody who knew what Danielle had achieved would rightly tell her to hold her head up high as they applauded her for having made a difference.

She might not have saved as many dogs as she would have liked, but then no one ever can.

chapter 9

Torture

The pain was unbearable.

Socks howled. He had never experienced anything like it.

The man with the neatly trimmed beard was a stocky guy, and his bear-like grip around Socks's midriff and neck ensured no matter how much Socks tried to bite and snap at his captor, he only succeeded in biting thin air.

The younger of his attackers laughed as he roughly grabbed hold of Socks's remaining large, soft ear with one hand and, in one obviously well-practised movement, used a butcher's knife in the other hand to chop it clean off, almost to the bone.

Socks howled again.

Docking a dog's ear is a brutal yet centuries-old Afghan tradition of the Kuchis. These nomadic tribes relied on the beautiful and strong Kuchi dog to protect their encampments from bandits or wolves while they slept. The mostly three- or four-strong dog pack that travelled alongside the caravan of camels and Kuchi tribespeople were loyal and fierce protectors of their adopted family. And, in return, the dogs' role was regarded as the vitally important job it was. Ensuring the dogs had eaten first, every day, was a priority for all family members.

But the Kuchi dogs were renowned for their substantial floppy ears and enormous fluffy tails. And large ears and tails make easy targets for an attacking wolf. In the case of an injury, especially to a ripped or torn ear, the nomads, with no access to any form of veterinary clinic, would struggle to stem bleeding and stop infection spreading in their beloved dogs – the medicines they used were mainly herbal-based remedies.

So a very straightforward solution was implemented for a very practical purpose: at birth, the ears of all the Kuchi pups were docked. While horrific to contemplate, it could actually save the dog a world of pain in later life: it was a 'when' and not an 'if' that the Kuchi dog pack would be called upon to defend their nomadic family.

But that tradition had been twisted and abused by a minority of the Afghan community, who supported the growing sport of dog fighting as an entertainment spectacle. They didn't want their combatants sporting any weakness going into battle, so ears and tail were removed, always without any form of painkillers, as early on in the dog's life as possible.

Which meant that Socks was being groomed for battle.

The pain surging from both sides of his head where, seconds earlier, his beautiful ears had been, caused the very distressed Socks to thrash fiercely, his head jerking violently from side to side as he mustered every fibre in his being in his attempt to escape from the abuse.

The man holding him cursed loudly as he lost his grip on Socks's neck. Fearing he was about to be mauled by the snarling dog, he used his arm around the dog's waist to propel the animal forcefully away from himself.

The younger man had moved to one side to be clear of the danger posed by the injured, flailing animal, but now was inadvertently in the direct path of the flung dog. Wide-eyed and now scared himself, he automatically flung up his arms to push the dog away, completely forgetting he was still holding the long-bladed knife.

Pain came again instantly as the tip of the knife sunk into Socks's white-blazed chest. Dropping to the floor like a brick, he landed with a thud on the hard concrete floor, the blood that spurted from the wound staining his once proud chest red.

Both men had stepped back from the stunned dog, the bigger man moving to a jug of water at the side of the room to rinse his hands and arms from the blood that had squirted from the cropped mess that remained of Socks's ears. The young man gave a wide berth around the crumpled heap of dog on the floor as he, too, made his way to the water jug.

Socks immediately took the opportunity to dart towards the open wooden door and away from the nightmare of pain he had found himself in. But in his confused and pained state, he had completely forgotten about the noose rope secured around his neck. As he sprinted away, the rope snapped taut against the concrete bollard he had been tied to. Socks was pole-axed in mid gallop, flipping over to land painfully on his back, blood once more oozing from the stab wound to his chest.

He lay there dazed for a few seconds before he screamed out once more as the pain returned him to the moment. He squirmed to his feet before hysterically straining and jerking against the rope that held him in a bid to break free, but he only pulled the noose tighter around his neck, restricting the air he needed to breathe.

It was no use. He could not escape. He was terrified.

Socks eyed his two attackers carefully as he lay on the floor, blood matted into the hair on the sides of his head and chest, gasping for as much breath as he could get. Luckily, as he lay still, the noose around his neck eased slightly.

The larger of the shabbily dressed Afghan men had finished cleaning off the splattered blood now, and grabbed the knife from the now shaking younger man.

Before Socks had registered that he had to move, the stern-faced Afghan grabbed his fine, fluffy tail that danced through the air on any other given day but which was now firmly down between his hind legs.

Once more the pain returned.

Socks couldn't understand why these men were doing this – he had only been looking for food.

Socks hadn't seen the kind old lady for several weeks now. He had made the journey every day to be fed from the same stainless-steel dish piled high with rice and naan bread. He knew that when the old lady with the kindly blue eyes did reappear that she would have some chicken hidden in her hand. She always played that game. And he never wanted the fuss she gave, once he had eaten, to end. He adored the human interaction.

But, recently, sitting patiently outside the large brown gate as the chill wind whipped up the alley, ruffling his long, out-of-control fur, he had waited in vain for the metallic sounds of the heavy bolts being slid free, the signal that the old lady was about to appear, carefully carrying his plate of food.

In fact, the old lady had failed to appear at all.

Each day Socks had waited for as long as he could but, eventually, hunger had sent him reluctantly away to search for another source of food.

And that was how he had come to be lying bloodied and bruised on the filthy floor, trembling in pain and wholly confused. He had wandered into an area of the city that he had never visited before, having exhausted his favourite list of possible places to find something to eat. But the edible garbage in the areas surrounding his normal stamping ground had been picked clean already.

The dried mud walls lining the unpaved streets had been considerably more crumbled and cracked than elsewhere in Kandahar. The houses were unkempt, and bullet holes adorned almost all the frontage. He had been on full alert for signs of a resident pack that would, no doubt, roam those streets. Last time had been too close for comfort.

He had spied the men from a distance. Warily, he had watched them as they sat chatting outside an isolated building, the sun bleaching the front wall and casting warmth over the two figures seated cross-legged on a carpet laid on the ground, engrossed in conversation while they ate rice from a large plate.

One of the men, a younger man with a long, black beard, had seen the curious young dog quietly watching the two of them and had thrown some rice in his direction.

Socks hadn't believed his luck. Throwing caution to the wind, he had happily trotted over to sniff the grains of rice lying on the dusty road. Like a hoover, he had sucked up each piece, his nose automatically sniffing out the whereabouts of the last grain.

More rice had been thrown but not so far this time, and Socks had gleefully continued to clean up, relishing the opportunity to eat.

He had no longer been paying any attention to the two men and hadn't noticed that the stockier of the two had stood up and moved as if to flank him.

The last handful of rice, thrown just to the side of the carpet, had suckered him right in to the terrifying trap in which he now found himself.

The dirty floor was cool against his pain-wracked body. Blood mixed with the dust of ages pooled at his sides. The pain was not subsiding as, wearily, Socks tried to stand to make a final attempt to escape from the rope that held him.

It was no use. He was too weak.

The man responsible for the crude docking of his tail untied the long leash holding Socks, before dragging the badly injured dog outside. Socks stumbled continuously as he was jerked by his neck, unable to keep pace with the striding Afghan in his faded blue jeans and black padded jacket. Now and again he would collapse to the ground but the man never slowed and just dragged Socks along until the desperate dog could once more regain his feet.

The corner of a building loomed up ahead and the Afghan led Socks, still bleeding and stumbling, into a much wider alley.

Socks could hear men jeering and yelling. And the sounds of dogs barking and growling. For the final time he tried resisting the man's pull by digging in his heels and hoping the rope would break from the man's tight grip. But he was too weak and the Afghan did not even break stride as Socks continued to be dragged towards whatever hell he faced next.

It didn't take long for him to find out. The beatings came quickly. The wooden poles struck his already battered body repeatedly as the three or four perpetrators cheered. Socks howled in pain again.

But, just as suddenly as the attack had started, it stopped.

Socks just lay on the filthy ground, exhausted. The battered dog, blood once more staining the ground around him red, waited for whatever horrible act was coming his way next.

But if he had opened his eyes, he would have seen his attackers running away from his bloodied body, the discarded beating sticks tossed aside as they ran. In their place, men with olive-drab uniforms were taking up positions either side of him, their weapons pointing outwards, away from him.

As they cleared the area surrounding him, they continued to move in the direction the Afghans had been headed, walking fast, continually watching their arcs, their weapons pulled in tight to their shoulders as their heads and rifle moved as one.

Socks felt somebody prodding his body. A voice near to him called out: 'Is it alive?'

'Yeah, boss. Just.'

'Seriously? Well, we can't just leave it there,' another voice joined in.

The first soldier nodded as he surveyed the scene. 'Roger that. Let's get him to the vehicle.'

Socks only partially acknowledged he was being lifted. The pain was numbing and he struggled to keep his eyes open.

The soldier carrying him walked slowly, mindful of the poor state the dog was in. As carefully as he could, he lowered the bleeding and almost unconscious dog onto a rough-textured blanket hastily thrown over the back seat of the vehicle.

'Don't worry, fella. We're going to get you some help. We know just the person.'

chapter 10

Never Quit

The text message had been brief but gave Danielle all the info she needed to know that it was probably going to be a long night.

She was moving as fast as she could. The customised animal first-aid pack she had slung around her body was annoyingly thumping up and down on her back as she ran, but she didn't have time to slow and adjust it. The message had said she needed to get to the entry checkpoint ASAP.

The colonel who had sent the message was already waiting at the checkpoint when she arrived. His humvee was parked behind him, the engine idling with the driver waiting patiently behind the wheel. One of the rear doors was open.

'Hey, Danielle, got a patient for you. But I am warning you, he looks bad.' The colonel already knew of Danielle's legendary animal welfare reputation – there were not many serving on Kandahar airfield who didn't. And he was most definitely a supporter.

He turned and reached into the back of the humvee. When

he turned back to face Danielle, she couldn't help herself: 'Oh my God!' she exclaimed, in sheer horror.

The colonel held a matted bundle of blood in his arms. Danielle immediately reached across as carefully as she could to take the mangled package from him.

'What happened to him?' Danielle was already trying to assess the dog's injuries, but there was too much congealing blood to distinguish what was what. She struggled to tell if the dog was even breathing.

'We were patrolling out in Kandahar when we came across some locals in an area they shouldn't have been, bashing the hell out of this little guy with clubs,' the colonel explained.

Still wearing his full combat gear, rifle hung by his side, the officer looked mean and very tired, as everybody around the base did. Not a good combination. Witnessing the attack on Socks was just another nail in the, 'What the hell are we doing in Afghanistan?' debate that was held most nights in the officers' mess.

He shook his head. 'Maybe they were riling him up for a fight, or using him as bait to train other dogs. Who knows?' he added wearily. 'But I couldn't just leave him like that. Stopping my corporal from shooting his attackers was hard enough.' He smiled for the first time since meeting Danielle.

'Oh, you poor baby,' Danielle said to the injured dog.

'Let me know how it goes. Gotta run, OK?' The colonel left Danielle cradling the dog.

Danielle didn't even notice the humvee pull away.

She had never seen anything like it. There was blood everywhere.

Mindful of not jolting the dog in her arms, she quickly carried her patient across to the sheltered area they used for caring and treating the clinic animals. She lowered him slowly to the ground before rifling through her medical pack to find a pair of surgical gloves.

Looking up, she saw with relief, arriving right on cue, two of the off-duty medics who also volunteered at the animal welfare clinic by the entrance to the airfield. Whilst both were highly trained combat medics more used to patching up soldiers on the battlefield, the principles were the same and they too, like Danielle, were shocked at the state of the dog before them.

Between them they set to work on Socks, starting out with cleaning and bathing the serious-looking puncture wound to his chest, before then checking him for broken bones and cleaning up the jagged tears where his ears had once been attached to his head.

The tail was chopped off a quarter of the way along what would have been its original length. 'Cruel bastards,' was a comment heard many times as they worked untiringly to save the dog, each one of them desperately attempting to control their emotions and the anger that they felt towards the men that had done this.

They worked long into the night: they doubted very much whether the dog would pull through. With his laboured breathing and the amount of blood he seemed to have lost, all three of his carers feared the worse.

They could only guess at any internal injuries he may have.

When they could do no more and there was a large pile of discarded dressing wrappers and blood-stained cotton balls by the comatose dog, Danielle sat down by the side of the ground sheet on which they had placed the dog in an attempt to keep his him off the dusty ground. A freshly washed towel had been wrapped delicately around his body to keep him warm.

They had managed to clean most of the matted blood from his long, brindled hair. Drying him, though, had been extremely difficult as he was bruised and clearly still in pain – with no access to anaesthetic, the pain must have been unbearable, but miraculously not once had the dog tried to bite or even growl at his saviours.

His white chest, now more pinkish than white, sported a clean, shaven patch that had allowed the access they needed to suture the stab wound properly. Danielle tucked the towel tighter around the dozing dog. 'Look at your cute little socked feet.' She spoke soothingly to the semi-conscious dog as she carefully ran a finger along the top of his head. 'And with that white hair on your chest, I guess that makes you look like Wylie Coyote.'

Socks actually did look very much like the Wylie Coyote cartoon character.

'Yeah. Wylie. That sound's a good name for you.'

And Socks gained his name, just like that.

'I bet, Wylie, you have a story to tell, little man,' Danielle continued running her finger through the damp hair on the top of his head, keeping well away from the trimmed areas around his ears, where they had done their best to seal and cover the wounds.

The soothing effect of Danielle's hands gently massaging his scalp sent Wylie into a deep sleep.

Danielle stayed like that for a while longer, feeling the weight of his battered body pressing into her legs as the dog finally relaxed, the painkillers and stress of whatever the hell had happened to him too much for him to fight. He needed the sleep.

'You are one lucky dog, Wylie,' she whispered, as she quietly stood up. She had to be back on duty soon.

She hoped he would make it through the night.

chapter 11

In the Wars Again

As April marched in and on, the days were definitely getting warmer. The sun now perched high above the mountains raised the mercury to knock on the door of the mid twenties. And that was enough to make it extremely uncomfortable if you happened to be doing military-type stuff.

Danielle was continuing her role as mentor to the Afghan police each day, but when the rest of the military day-shift headed back to their accommodation for some well-deserved down time, she would be gearing up to begin her self-appointed second job as the dog rescuer of Kandahar.

It was becoming an exhausting routine.

Just as animal lovers the world over agreed; sleep was an overrated commodity when you had animals to rescue. Especially when it meant you could make a difference, as they had done for the dog with the four white-socked feet that they had named Wylie.

The battered fluffball had beaten the odds and survived that first night, which no one could quite believe – Danielle and the team looking after him had been amazed when they had seen his cropped tail wagging slowly from side to side as they had arrived the next morning to check on him and change the dressings.

And, gradually, over the course of the following days, even being somewhat unsteady on his feet at first, the plucky dog had ventured out to explore the surroundings of the checkpoint.

The amazing thing was that Wylie would happily allow soldiers who he had never met before to ruffle the top of his head. After all he had been through, Wylie seemed to grasp just who the good guys were.

But the lovable dog did seem to lack some common sense, and that almost proved to be his downfall again. The dog was a 'hurt locker' magnet all of his own.

Danielle received the unwelcome call at three in the morning from the duty watch on the checkpoint.

Anyone listening, if they hadn't known these soldiers better might actually have thought the caller was struggling to hold back tears.

Wylie had taken himself off for a late-night stroll away from the protective cordon of the checkpoint but had, once more, ended up in the wrong hands. The 'who' was not really clear, but the 'what' was plain for all to see.

The soldiers at the checkpoint had found Wylie hobbling back to the safety they provided, blood gushing from his belly and a deep gash across his lip and down the side of his chin.

Scrambling for their first-aid supplies, the checkpoint watch crew had done their best to stem the flow of blood.

And it was with anger and disbelief that the soldiers had found that the severely bleeding injury on the dog's belly was more horrendous than they had assumed.

They had discovered a deep slice wound to his penis. The soldiers had been shocked. They could not believe that somebody would actually attempt to sever a dog's penis. Wylie had, by some miracle, clearly managed to struggle free before whoever holding him had had the chance to finish the gruesome job.

The battle-toughened soldiers, who thought they had seen it all, realised that life had yet more lessons for them.

Danielle and the team had believed they had already carried out the only emergency surgery Wylie would ever need. But, seizing the surgical supplies they presumed would be needed, they came together a second time to save him.

Once more crouched over on the hard ground atop a blue medical drape, by the side of a concrete suicide-vehicle stopper-block to help keep the dust and dirt at bay, Danielle prepared to restrain Wylie with a beige, oddly fashioned muzzle of sorts from a piece of medical strapping – just in case – as he lay flat on his back.

Wearing his traditional *salwar kameez* and at times looking completely out of place amongst the doting, camouflaged personnel surrounding the injured dog, Aseel was by now part of Wylie's personal and experienced combat medical team. He had volunteered immediately to help Danielle with the treatment as soon as he had received the text stating that she needed help.

Together, the team operated by the light of a torch held by a soldier sitting off to one side in the cramped surroundings of an airfield mortar shelter as the Taliban did their best to lob 107mm rockets onto the base. The confined surroundings of the darkened shelter was admittedly not the best place for this type of thing, but Danielle's team had no other choice. Wylie needed lifesaving treatment and he needed it immediately. The deep wound had to be closed, as he would probably not survive an infection if he picked one up, and Danielle did not have the drugs to treat something like that. Out in Afghanistan, infections tended to be on the aggressive side.

Carrying out the surgery under the pre-fabricated concrete bunker that simply consisted of two sides, a roof and a concrete bollard chicane to get into the protective space, was the safest place to be. In the event of a close impact by a 107mm shell it would probably save their lives, although their hearing would suffer for a few days after, most likely.

But concern for their own safety was not an issue amongst the dedicated team as they cleaned, stitched and cared for the innocent dog that had just been in the wrong place at the wrong time. All were focused on the task at hand of saving a dog's life. As far as they were concerned, the Taliban could wait.

To some of the soldiers and contractors at the airfield, it was an incomprehensible notion. Not being dog people, they struggled to understand what drove Danielle's team to forget their own welfare and be that dedicated to aiding a mangy stray dog whilst the Taliban attempted to kill them all. But to those trying to save Wylie, it was as natural as breathing. When they needed to be soldiers they were; but soldiers could still care for the innocents of war, and that was what they were doing now.

As before, everyone working on his injuries was amazed by Wylie's ability to endure the procedures without complaint. The dog that had been through more pain than any dog should ever suffer lay there still and unmoving as the medics and Aseel worked on him. It was as if he could distinguish between pain for good and pain for bad. As before, and to the relief of everyone, the strap Danielle held loosely as a muzzle was ultimately a precaution rather than a necessity.

Wylie seemed relaxed and content snuggled on his back, locked in place by Danielle's legs, his two front paws facing up to the sky as if he was begging for another bone, whilst his rear legs were held gently outstretched by another soldier so that the medic and Aseel could work in the crook of his belly.

All seemed to go well, but the medics warned that this dog with nine lives would need to see a 'real' vet at some point; that what they had done for him was probably only a temporary measure. But they all agreed it would do him for now.

In fact, the team of acting dog medics was required to operate four times to repair the damage done. The knife had caused an injury that was understandably incredibly difficult to treat.

Danielle's reputation, whilst receiving accolades from across the base for her dog rescue dedication, was starting to lose its appeal when it came to donations.

The cost of transporting Lady's newly adopted pups had been pretty substantial, and whilst Danielle herself donated heavily, she still had to go cap in hand time and time again to whoever she could find that had expressed even a remote interest in what she was doing. She was given a short brief respite from her fund raising nightmare when the soldier who had generously decided to take on Lady and give her a home in Colorado also offered to pay the full fees associated with the transportation costs, it was a small success for which Danielle was grateful.

But she was not alone in the problem she now faced. Just like animal shelter workers across the world experienced day in day out, Danielle and her team would rehome one pup, celebrate that success briefly and then *boom*, another desperately needy pup would arrive to fill the puppy vacuum that the band of Kandahar dog rescuers had only just celebrated creating!

Danielle's work had unwittingly unleashed a beast. As more people heard about this fanatical animal rescuer, more puppies started arriving, plucked from the streets.

Ultimately, the generosity of the military staff from Danielle's captive pool at Kandahar airfield started to wear thin.

Adding to the strain, Wylie, if he kept true to his current form, would probably not survive much longer: he would at some point run out of lives. Everyone had become so attached to the brindled fluffball whilst patching him up that they knew they would never be completely happy unless he was safely in a loving home. And there was one place Danielle could guarantee that.

Australia, and *her* home.

Calculating the costs on a piece of scrap paper, the black-inked figures coldly announcing that it would take months to raise the money required to fund a one-way trip to Australia for the dog that was slowly becoming part of her life.

Complicating the issue, and no matter how much she re-arranged the figures, Australia had some of the strictest animal import regulations in the world to contend with. Coming from a rabies-endemic country like Afghanistan meant Wylie would be required to undergo quarantine for six months in another, officially approved country, before he could even enter Australia. He would be on his own for those long six months, and Danielle couldn't keep flying to another country to visit him.

Added to all this, you had to doubt that the happy-go-lucky mutt would still be around to even get on the flight. There was no way of containing him while she endeavoured to raise the impossible amount of money that was needed.

To save Wylie necessitated outside help. And Danielle knew, thankfully, just who she needed to reach out to.

chapter 12

Dear Pen

I read the email one more time on my home computer, which doubled as my office work station. The subject line simply stated: 'Rescue Request'.

It started 'Dear Pen', and whilst that in itself was nothing out of the ordinary, it always felt slightly weird that complete strangers knew who I was. Not 'Dear Sir or Madam' but 'Pen'.

I really did struggle at times to grasp the enormity of the task I had created for myself. The very surreal responsibilities that came with managing an animal welfare charity that operated in war-torn Afghanistan were at times, overwhelming to say the least. 'What the hell have I started?' was a thought that could often be found lurking in the dark recesses of my brain.

Actually, more often than not, these days.

Of all the places in the world that I could have unintentionally chosen to become the focal point for dog rescue, I had chosen Afghanistan – currently the most dangerous place on earth on for a westerner, next to Baghdad in Iraq. What was I *thinking*?!

Whilst I had been serving as a Royal Marine Commando, animal welfare had been the furthest thing from my mind, to be honest. For those that have served will know, a military career can be fairly limiting in all aspects of one's life, outside the 'green' job. My one passion had been rock climbing and all the outdoor adventure that I could squeeze in around crawling through the undergrowth in a far-off place attempting to sneak up behind an unsuspecting enemy. The brief and always far too short trips to climb soaring rock faces on remote peaks were my sole focus away from the regimented and very much orderly world of the armed forces.

Balanced delicately on tiptoes, barely standing on the slimiest of granite edges as my fingertips sought out the faintest protruding nodule of rock so I could continue moving fluently upwards, hundreds of feet of nothing below me, found me most definitely in my element. When I was at the sharp end of the rope, leading a long run-out pitch that required all of my skill and effort just to stay in contact with the smooth rock wall . . . that was when I felt most completely in control of my life. There was nobody else to help me or do it for me. It was just me against the rock. I loved the physicality of the focus it commanded, and I was happy to give it my undivided attention.

Being married to a sea-going Wren had worked well, as she had completely understood my desire to get away and climb. Our military backgrounds had meant we were well used to time apart from each other and, like hundreds of military families around the globe, we just got on with it.

Our two dogs, Fizzdog, the people-loving Rottweiler, and Beamerboy, the mad as a bag of rabbits rescued Springer spaniel, lived on the various military camps with us. We juggled our, at times, very hectic lives around long dog walks, a social beer or two and the very demanding commitments of the military senior ranks we held.

But my deployment with 42 Commando Royal Marines to Afghanistan changed all of that. And it didn't stop with just my life: the ripples from my tour in Afghanistan seem to have changed the lives of so many other people, too.

And that I truly struggle to get my head around.

The Helmand Province market town of Now Zad, nestled at the southern tip of the Hindu Kush mountains, was meant to be business as usual for those of us tasked with defending the remote forward operating base that we called home for nearly three months. We had trained continually for nearly a year for every eventuality we would likely encounter during our deployment to Afghanistan. Our mission was simple: to provide security to the local Afghan people and disrupt the Taliban ambition to return to power. And that, as far as I was concerned, was what I, along with the Royal Marines of Five Troop, Kilo Company, would endeavour to do.

But I hadn't counted on the feelings of helplessness I would experience towards the hungry stray dogs I would see through the telescopic sights of my weapon as I took my turn manning one of the many sentry posts that had to be occupied 24 hours a day. The feral dogs would roam outside our desert compound, wandering aimlessly, constantly scavenging for food. To me it was heart-wrenching stuff just watching them. With no one to care for them and no loving homes to go to, the dogs were born to a short and mostly very cruel life.

I don't recall seeing any old dogs during my time in Now Zad. Disease, the extreme climate and starvation made sure of that.

We had been warned that the night-time temperature could drop a fair bit, making it unpleasant at times whilst manning the sentry positions. So we had come prepared, with our issued thermal undies to don, but to a man none of us had really appreciated just how bloody cold it could be. A mind-numbing –25°C took us all by surprise – the skin of your bare finger could stick instantly to the metal of your rifle should you have a lapse of concentration and pick up your weapon without the protection of gloves.

For a street dog, already hungry and weak, the chances of surviving the onslaught of the Afghan winter were pretty remote. And, as if to rub salt in the wound, there was always the popular practice of dog fighting to decrease the odds of survival even further.

Man has, over the countless centuries we have been on this planet, come up with many unsavoury activities with which to amuse himself, normally with a complete disregard for all other species. Regrettably, dog fighting in Afghanistan is one such barbaric activity that continues to flourish unabated.

In fact, I had been surprised to read in my research, prior to being deployed, that dog fighting was banned under the rule of the Taliban, their leadership firmly declining to tolerate it. Added to this, all contact with dogs was outlawed, and the punishment was harsh by any standards. However, I had concluded that they didn't ban dog fighting because the Taliban leadership were dedicated animal welfare activists and, as I had assumed, that was indeed far from the case. The Taliban interpretation of the Koran decrees that dogs are regarded as dirty animals and extremely un-Islamic – being caught handling or owning a dog resulted in a public flogging. Which, spookily enough, was the universal punishment for most crimes under Taliban governance.

When the Taliban was finally declared as being defeated by the United States government on 30 January 2002, dog fighting had, sadly, immediately begun to gain popularity once more.

At first, the dog fights were held in the remote and often lawless provinces far away from the authority of Kabul, but soon the mainly male-dominated society demanded more access to the brutal, so-called entertainment and, alas, it began to creep back gradually into the major towns and cities spread across Afghanistan, too.

And, much to my horror, I realised that dog fighting could be profitable. I was amazed by the money swirling around the dog-fighting scene, especially for a country rated the third poorest in the world. A prized Afghan Kuchi dog, a distant relative of the Anatolian Shepard dog, with its ears cropped brutally close to the side of its large stocky head, was savage in the ring but, out of it, a gentle giant. It could also be worth US$50,000 or more.

Friday afternoon, after prayers, would see hundreds of adult Afghan men clustered around two battling beasts in a cloud of kicked-up dust as the dogs ripped into one another, teeth clashing as their primitive instincts to be the alpha dog came snarling to the surface.

A fight would only end when there was a clearly dominant victor.

Thankfully, I had read that some elements of the Afghan government were keen for dog fighting to be firmly outlawed, due to its un-Islamic nature and of the logical connection that its popularity fuelled gambling addiction and debt amongst the Afghan lower classes, which was steadily becoming a problem that had to be dealt with.

But, although dog fighting was technically illegal, according to the Afghan statute books, apparently too many of the rich and powerful in Afghanistan actively involved themselves in the 'sport' and so little was done to stem the tide of what most civilised folks would call a barbaric and cruel pastime.

I was very much of the opinion of gathering up all those responsible for organising the unsightly spectacle of dog fighting across Afghanistan and, under a tournament of our own, make the former organisers fight. But I guessed that that way of thinking, whilst maybe popular with the animal welfare activists, probably wouldn't ever see the light of day.

The Taliban did act once, in January 2008, killing two birds with one stone as it were by directing a suicide bomber to target Abdul Hakim Jan, a former provincial police chief who had previously stood up to the Taliban, as he attended a dog fight on the outskirts of Kandahar. The resulting explosion and confusion also caused the deaths of over eighty spectators as, in sheer panic, the official's bodyguards, dazed and confused, opened up with their assault rifles into the mass of unsuspecting attendees scrambling to flee the kill zone in a disastrous attempt to kill attackers who, by all accounts, were already dead. A further ninety people, according to the local hospitals, had been injured.

The Taliban had released a press announcement claiming responsibility for the attack and confirming the illegality of dog fighting under their charter, showing no remorse for the killings of the innocent bystanders.

Simply put, the Taliban said they should not have been there.

During my time in Helmand, I understood I wasn't going to stop dog fighting; nor did I think I could do anything for the many hungry strays that roamed around the outside of our compound. But what *could* I do for them? I constantly asked myself this as the frustration at being completely powerless to intervene in their desperate plight ate away at me every time I took up my sentry duty, the feral dogs casting a sorrowful backdrop to my watch for the next Taliban attack.

I most definitely hadn't counted on witnessing a dog fight first-hand in that remote firebase. It had started innocently enough – a gathering of men, laughing and joking – but I had soon realised that the group was actually forcing two dogs to fight right there in front of me. I had been nothing short of appalled. It was a horrific sight as the two dogs engaged in a ferocious battle.

Without hesitation, I'd forced my way in to stop the fight organised by our own Afghan police contingent that was co-located with us. It was simple economics: our guns were bigger than those the Afghan police carried.

And we were, without question, more passionate about our cause than they were. It was a fight they most definitely would not have won, nor had had the stomach for.

One of the dogs, his closely cropped ears still red-raw from the brutal procedure, the open gashes from the recent fight clearly etched into the right side of his face, had sought sanctuary in our compound.

I couldn't blame him. He had had nowhere else to go.

He had looked scrawny and extremely scared, and I figured he just wanted to be left alone. Which was all well and good, but I couldn't be sure he wouldn't bite any of my lads if they stumbled across him or tried to interact with him at some point. Nor would my direct boss, the officer commanding the forward operating base, have tolerated it for a start, had he known.

No, the tan-coloured, Alsatian-looking dog had to go. But he was reluctant to let me get too close in my fumbled attempts at removing him from the compound. My attempt at a wheedling, 'Come on, buddy. I'm not going to hurt you,' succeeded in me only securing a warning growl in reply. I figured it was a precursor to the nasty bite I would receive if I pursued my attempts to drag him from his bolt-hole hidden away in the narrow disused storeroom – I didn't need any other indicators to reinforce the message that I should back away. Slowly.

Over the course of the next several days, as I attempted to seek his trust, the cardboard-tasting military biscuits my main source of mediation between us, something happened.

That mangy-looking mutt became my four-legged companion and, I guessed, I became the first human to ever show him kindness.

I soon realised that coaxing him outside our metal compound gates so I could slam them shut on him, expecting that he would then just saunter off down the mud-walled alley to face whatever a dog's life was going to throw at him, was not going to happen.

I knew I had over-stepped the boundary when the former fighting dog gained his first ever name. It wasn't difficult.

'How does the name Nowzad sound to you?' I had asked the docked-eared stray sitting between my legs. As I looked down at him, there was a clear resemblance to the war-torn and scarred town we were fighting over.

He just ate another biscuit. The constant supply of biscuits had probably ensured he wasn't going anywhere any time soon.

'Guess you get to stay, eh, Nowzad?' I mused, as I fed him another bit.

I wasn't ashamed to admit that I pretty much needed him as much as he needed me. He was my five minutes of respite each day, a magic carpet that lifted me away to a place that was not the confined and restrictive bullet-magnet life in the Now Zad district compound.

To state that we were both now the only positive aspects of each other's daily lives probably wasn't far from the truth.

And so I rescued Nowzad.

I still to this day struggle to understand just how the seemingly random aspects of the plan all fitted together, almost seamlessly, to see Nowzad arrive in quarantine in England and then, six months later, my home.

But although by then I was no longer serving in Afghanistan, I could not quite shake the country from my waking thoughts. As a soldier, you either return from the front lines and just get on with your life, the time spent on deployment just part of the job you joined up for – 'No biggy' as the lads used to say; or you leave a bit of yourself in that far-off place, and being back home, doing the everyday stuff that most people do on autopilot, just doesn't feel quite right. Walking around a supermarket when only a few days earlier you were being mortared is, simply, indescribable.

We had lost two of our Marines in Helmand and having five of them return home with life-changing injuries affected me, deep down. I didn't feel the guilt that some lads experience that they have come home but their mates didn't; it was different. I just couldn't understand how we came home at the end of our deployment, having given so much, without finishing what we had started. Not for years after our time in Afghanistan would the benefits of the military intervention and determination to support the Afghan people start to be seen by the outside world.

Of course, as soldiers, we only saw our blinkered view of the coalition's mission in Afghanistan. We never got to the see the whole picture. Not many do – not even the politicians who started it in the first place, like Bush. It was left up to his successor to mop things up.

But I was impatient.

I had to do something as soon as I could.

And, looking at a newly arrived Nowzad, curled up content and with a full belly under my desk, I knew it meant going back to Afghanistan. And that was, simply, how the Nowzad Dogs charity had started.

The main focus of the charity was delivering quality animal welfare treatment and providing a rescue shelter for the street dogs of Kabul. It soon expanded to include assisting soldiers rescue and repatriate the companion animals they had befriended.

At first, during the summer of 2007, the Nowzad Dogs HQ operated out of my spare bedroom: naively, I hadn't considered how the charity would eventually expand. 'I will deal with that when we get there,' was my simple solution, when asked. But I had not counted on the charity exploding due to the amazing support we started to receive from day one.

The connection between soldiers on the front lines in Afghanistan and the defenceless companion animals they adopted had become an instant hit with the public, and pretty soon the charity became too big to manage. I knew we needed to expand.

Initially, I attempted to expand the scope of the charity without really spending any time thinking through all the implications – time that would have been well spent.

Hindsight is a wonderful afterthought.

I had thousands of crazy plans for implementing animal welfare in Afghanistan and, slowly, bit by bit and without me realising, managing the charity became my all-encompassing obsession. Sucked into the world of charity admin, I failed to realise that my drive and passion was not also my wife's. And it didn't help that we lost the glue that had bound us together for many years: Fizzdog, the rascal Rottie, died after a lengthy battle from throat cancer.

The feeling of complete devastation when I took the call from the vet was brutal. To this day I still can't think of Fizzdog without feeling incredibly sad.

The divorce saw me lose Beamerboy, too.

But, of course, Nowzad and my other two Afghan rescues, Tali and Patchdog, came to live with me. Renting a remote, one-bedroom cottage in Cornwall that had once been used as the office for the start of the UK arm of Animals Asia, an international charity that campaigns hard for the abolishment of bear bile farming in China, a horrific practice that resulted in the elegant 'Moon bears' being permanently imprisoned for most of their lives in tiny cages. The charity was making good progress too, its founder Jill Robinson a force to be reckoned with in her drive to give the bears their freedom back.

Soon my cramped cottage became even cosier as the four of us were soon joined by a seriously mad dog called Maxchat.

Max's story was complicated. A British soldier in Iraq had made the horrifying discovery of Iraqi guards in Baghdad swinging a month-old puppy around by its tail. He had intervened on impulse. The Nowzad Dogs charity had reached out to Iraq and rescued the puppy for the soldier's family.

Max had lasted two weeks in their family home. He had been too unpredictable and they couldn't give him the time needed for training. He was dumped back at the quarantine they had only recently collected him from.

With no network of fosters or adopters in place for such a scenario, I had done the only thing I could think of: Max became known as Maxchat and moved in to join my pack in our now very crowded countryside retreat.

Since then, the charity has spawned a network of new friends around the globe, all passionate about the dogs and cats of Afghanistan who have no voice but ours. The upshot has been the unlikely scenario of me ending up with two published books to my name – and masses of publicity for the charity from local and national press.

And the fact that my name became synonymous with rescuing dogs in Afghanistan.

I briefly scrolled though the two pages of the email. An Australian police officer wanted us to help her rescue a dog called Wylie from Kandahar and have him shipped to Australia.

I quickly replied with a short email more or less simply stating: 'No problems. I will come back to you with some details.'

Whilst we had never rescued a dog for an Australian before, I didn't really have any doubts that importing a dog into Australia would give us any problems at all.

chapter 13

Baghdad Cat Lady

'Wylie, pack that in,' I said in a calm and relaxed voice, but just loud enough to be heard over his defiant barking. Wylie was standing solidly to attention, barking and staring fairly aggressively, just inches away from the chain-link fencing that separated him from his nemesis on the other side.

I was tired. Having only just arrived in Afghanistan, I was still feeling the effects of jet lag and it would take me several days to get used to the draining heat.

To be fair, Wylie's nemesis, a squat, tan-coloured dog called Peg, was not doing anything to calm things down but giving his all in snarling and yapping back.

'Good grief,' I muttered to nobody in particular.

My chilled voice had done nothing remotely by way of calming the two of them down. It was brutally hot, the sun burning any fair skin within minutes of being exposed; sun cream not being a commodity widely available in Kabul. I adjusted the baseball cap I was wearing on my forehead, a line of sweat already running down the side of my face. I wiped it off with the cloth sweat band I wore around my wrist.

'Seriously, will the two of you shut *up*!' I now yelled to be heard above the incessant barking. I was losing my patience. It was just too hot for this crap. They had been at it for ages, and it seemed neither dog was going to back down anytime soon.

'Wylie, stop that. Peg is special, remember?'

Wylie, to be fair, probably didn't know the story of Peg. He may have cut the dog some slack had he known.

Private Conrad Lewis of the Parachute Regiment had been befriended by Peg on the front lines in Helmand just a few months earlier. Her name 'Peg' was short for 'Pegasus', the winged emblem that the regiment is so proud of.

When I received a phone call from a bloke called Tony – who, it transpired, was Conrad's father – I had listened intently as he told me all about the dog and his son's tour of Helmand province.

Conrad had joined the reserves during his gap year before university studies, intent on ensuring he did his bit for his country. I commended his dedication and bravery – not many lads his age would have decided to do that, unless they were full-time regular army.

'Definitely deserves a pint should I happen to bump into him,' I thought to myself as I continued listening.

Tony paraphrased the letters written home by his son describing the antics of the dog and the morale boost the little brown-coloured scamp gave the lads of his troop. To those soldiers, living in the midst of a war they probably didn't know a lot about, Peg was a positive aspect they could focus on. Something real and comforting. Ensuring she survived was seriously more important to Conrad and his mates than anything else happening at that moment, and they were determined that Peg would be given a loving home in England.

So I knew where the call was going. Much like the other phone calls and emails we received, I assumed Tony was asking on behalf of his son if the charity could assist in rescuing the dog that they clearly could not bear to leave behind.

In that moment I learnt a serious lesson. I never pre-judge any phone call these days.

Tony had stopped talking. The line was quiet. He had yet to ask if the charity could rescue the dog.

'My son was killed by a Taliban sniper three weeks ago,' he simply stated.

Now it was my turn to go quiet. My brain raced to form a suitable reply. I felt completely inadequate.

The guy had lost his son.

I automatically thought back to the day I had stood in front of Marine Ben Reddy's mother as we repatriated his body to RAF Brize Norton, Ben having been killed by a Taliban bullet during our deployment in Helmand. In those brief seconds, as she had watched his coffin draped in the Union Jack being carefully carried on the shoulders of his comrades, I had had nothing to say to her. What do you say? There is no training or script for a moment like that. I had stood there desperately trying to hold back tears of my own. The troop sergeant is not meant to cry.

My mind had raced back to the moment in hand and the hurting father on the other end of the line. I had spluttered out an apology and then blurted out the only thing I could say in reply: 'Tony, we will find Peg and get her to your family.'

It wasn't until after I had put the phone receiver down that I realised we didn't even know where in Helmand Peg was.

But my worry was to be short-lived. Through old contacts, favours and the determination of our new shelter manager who had joined us towards the end of 2010, Louise, Peg had arrived at our animal sanctuary by means that are still sanctioned under the Official Secrets Act.

And whilst, like Wylie, Peg was a completely adorable dog who loved everyone when she was on her own, for some bizarre reason she couldn't stand Wylie and Wylie, who liked every other dog, couldn't stand Peg even though she was female.

They resumed their aggressive stance towards each other with passion, their barking going into overdrive. But I had a plan for eventualities like this.

The large bucket of cold water placed specifically by the rickety wooden gate that allowed access into Wylie's kennel run was heavy to lift at first, but once I had heaved it backwards and let momentum do the work for me as I swung it forward, the subsequent deluge of water sailed gracefully through the air to soak first Wylie from head to tail and then drench Peg, microseconds later.

The barking ceased immediately as, dripping water, Wylie and Peg struggled to grasp what had just happened.

As both dogs turned to look at me as if to ask, 'What the heck did you do that for?' I bent down to place the now empty red bucket down against the wonky gate.

Safiollah, our duty kennel staff member for the day, a short and always smiling Afghan from the Hazara tribes of the north-west, was already carrying over a replacement bucket just filled from the large, blue water tank that stood in the middle of the kennels, kept topped up weekly by deliveries from a local water company. A big grin came my way. He clearly knew the routine.

'I did warn you both,' I replied to the 'You're dead to me' silent treatment I was now getting from both dogs.

With great fanfare, both dogs gave themselves a typical dog shake from head to tail, water droplets sailing off into the distance, before they headed off to sit in the shade.

Quietly.

Lesson learnt, I assumed.

'Right, it's sorted!' I yelled over to Louise, who was busy preparing vaccines in the small cabin that doubled as our cat room.

'Yeah,' Louise shot back at me without turning her head, 'give them five minutes. You may want to stock up on buckets,' she continued, her deep Brummie accent at times completely baffling the Afghans. Dr Hadi, our head vet, had even once asked me if Louise was actually speaking in English.

Louise had filled the position of the full-time shelter manager that I so desperately needed when she had decided to give up the trappings of the well-paid security circuit to come on board with the Nowzad Dogs charity full time.

Building a proper animal shelter that the Nowzad charity could call home was her first order of the day.

I couldn't have hoped for a better candidate: Louise came with a pedigree in animal rescue already. From an on-off career in the Territorial Army, she had seen service in Iraq before the security industry had tempted her to jump ship and earn a small fortune each month living in remote and often very dangerous parts of Iraq, managing the staff of large-scale private security companies.

But, over the years of hard grind in the harsh landscape of an imploding Iraq, Louise had earned herself a very different title from that which the company she worked for had bestowed upon her. In fact, Louise had once been known as the 'Cat Lady of Baghdad', as newspapers had picked up on her one-woman mission to rescue as many of Iraq's feral cats and dogs as she could.

Her first rescue had not been intentional. A white cat with tabby-coloured patches on his skinny, underfed body, was found desperately in need of care. Louise had named it Simba al Tikriti, on account of her love of the film *The Lion King* and that the cat had been rescued from Saddam Hussein's home town of Tikrit.

Most of the non-military security staff based in Tikrit had been housed in a large, secure compound on the edge of the town, and an Iraqi cleaner called Mona had been employed to keep their accommodation in a reasonably tidy condition. Finding a half-dead cat out by the garbage near to where she lived, Mona had felt sympathy for the animal. She had attempted to care for it herself, concealing what she was up to so as not to make her husband aware of her actions, knowing full well that he would not approve. But he had found the cat anyway, and threatened to kill it.

Mona had remembered seeing colourful photos of obviously much-loved animals pinned to the wall in the western woman's room who worked for the security company that employed Mona. Mona, although she couldn't quite understand it, had even seen that woman talking to dogs and cats that had been pushed in front of a computer screen thousands of miles away in England! As if animals could understand what the crazy woman was saying!

The crazy woman who talked to animals was Louise.

Without any doubt, the best person to care for the cat was Louise who, one morning, found herself abruptly presented with a rubbish bag. A badly injured grey and white tabby cat had stared back at her from the bottom of the bag.

And so Louise had suddenly found herself the focal point

for other animal lovers caring for dogs and cats in the remote forward operating bases in the desolate interior of Iraq who needed her help in transporting their animals out of the battle-weary country. Pulling in favours, arguing with Iraqi officials and even risking her own life as she attempted to catch two escaped dogs; *Sandbag* and *Dirtbag*, around the dangerous streets of Baghdad without the normally essential protection offered by an accompanying security detail. Louise had set about making a real difference to the cats and dogs befriended in that war-torn slice of the world that nobody really cared too much about.

But, as the war machine in Iraq had begun to wind down then so, too, had the civilian security contracts. As the money and jobs began to move east to Afghanistan, so did Louise. But for her, it was not just the end of another security contract: the move had signalled the end of her Baghdad cat lady career.

As with most of us, who have no idea what fate has in store around the corner, Louise was no exception. Ultimately, her move was not the end of her rescuer's career: far from it. Within weeks of being in Kabul, she had heard that the Nowzad Dogs charity needed a full-time shelter manager with experience of managing Muslim staff and, more importantly, of course, animal rescue.

I always smile at the memory of when she asked me about the other candidates she had beaten to get the job. She had been the only candidate.

Louise seemed to prefer working and living full-time in Afghanistan and, at times, seemed loath to travel home to the United Kingdom. Not because she didn't want to see her mum and dad – far from it. She raved about the Tandoori chicken her mum would religiously have waiting for her when she arrived home from the airport – it had been her meal of choice for the previous ten years when she had arrived home in England from her long stints in Iraq. Louise loved going home, but she worried frantically for the animals she left behind in Afghanistan during what was meant to be her time off relaxing at home. The old adage of 'Nobody does your job better than you can do' was very pertinent to Louise's way of thinking.

I usually calculated that she had not been home long enough for the Tandoori to digest before my phone would start to resonate with the wacky 'Taliban Calling' ring tone I had keyed in for her number.

'Remember *Sherak* needs his medicine.'

'Remember to feed the cats.'

'Have you given *Portia* her tablets?'

I was meant to be giving Louise complete confidence that the dogs and cats would be just fine and dandy when I stepped into her shoes. But I had a sneaky feeling that she would not be happy with whoever was there to stand in for her. My former life as a Royal Marine sergeant responsible for thirty young, overly enthusiastic Marines was lost on Louise. Admittedly her cats were sometimes fed a little later than usual and not always the special cat food that she had hidden away, but eh, what she didn't know wouldn't hurt her. The animals were all still alive when she came back to Afghanistan, and that was what mattered. And when she returned to Kabul, her suitcases would always be laden with vital supplies for the shelter.

Louise handled the claustrophobic nature of being a western woman living and working in Afghanistan as best she could. Popping out to the shops for a pint of milk or heading off to browse the many colourful and thriving markets was out of the question – the unwanted attention of the mainly male shoppers put paid to that.

On one return from the UK, her comments about seeing more burkas on the high street back home than she did in Kabul actually had a ring of truth to it. We had both noticed that more and more women in Kabul were choosing to ditch the all-encompassing drab, blue burka, instead opting to venture out in skinny jeans – but even on the hottest of days, a normally long black coat covered any hint of a female figure. The *pièce de résistance* was just a headscarf wrapped loosely over the top of their jet-black, long hair, while the varying degrees of red lipstick were most definitely a sign of outward defiance at the restrictions of the past.

All this, in a society where women were previously aggressively hidden from every aspect of daily life, was a massive step forward and all thanks to the improving security in Afghanistan. With the improved and robust security now in place in Kabul and the other major cities, to some extent, the Afghans' confidence that they would no longer be subject to the previous extreme punishments the Taliban would mete out for any infringements of their strict version of Islam was growing, and people were starting to take the opportunities to express themselves. Wearing make-up for women, or not having a beard longer than fist-length from the base of the chin for men; anybody listening to music; anyone watching a movie; women laughing out loud as, under the Taliban, no woman's voice should have been heard in public . . . the list went on, and were offences that were punishable only one way under the Taliban justice system: a public whipping.

It was all down to the dedication of the coalition troops that had held back the Taliban long enough for the Afghan security forces to come up to speed to take over the reins of providing the nation's security; whereas in England, it seemed to us, more and more Muslim women seemed to be embracing the restrictive demands of wearing the *burka*, some, sadly, in support of the hard-line version of their religion, which they had never experienced first-hand.

The hardships of living in Kabul was, to Louise, the price she paid to make a difference to the animals she loved. In fact, she thrived on the day-to-day grind of extreme animal rescue that Afghanistan had to offer.

And I actually envied her. Big time.

My role within the charity, as I was technically the boss, meant that when I was back in the UK my desk would just scream paperwork at me. Piles of it. All charity-related and all needing answering. Yesterday. The annoying 'You have a new email' icon seemed to ping up on my computer screen every few minutes. And, without even looking, I would know who most of them were from.

Some days – no, I lie – most days I wished that Mr Tim Berners-Lee had messed up a line of computer code somewhere in the complex series of 0s and 1s he had put together, and the World Wide Web and, more importantly email, had stayed a far-fetched idea.

Text was now Louise's preferred method of contact, along with Skype, email, WhatsApp and the phone.

She was good at keeping in contact. While my email inbox was a mess of out-dated emails, emails needing replies, emails for forwarding and those I just hadn't even read, she stayed on top of her inbox easily. She also knew the state of play, and had obviously decided to circumnavigate my disorganisation by using another form of technology.

'Pen, you haven't replied to that email I sent you yesterday about those supplies for the shelter. YOU NEED TO RING ME NOW!' the text that had just arrived on my phone stated simply.

I slipped the phone back into my jacket pocket and zipped it up.

I stood up and, without checking my rope, leant out over the edge of the narrow belay ledge, 700 feet up the vertical rock walls of Ice Box Canyon. The climbing rope tied to the harness I was wearing went taut against the bolted belay anchors I had clipped.

I was leaning out at 45 degrees, looking out and down on to the most breath-taking scenic vista that Red Rocks National Park in Nevada, the good ole US of A, had to offer.

My climbing partner, renowned for being extremely enthusiastic – for his age – and one of the boss men at climbing wall builders, Entre Prises, was currently engaged in battle 80 feet below me with an extremely wide sandstone crack that required the leg-splits ability of a gymnast thirty years younger. But Mick was nailing the moves and moving steadily upwards as I took in the safety rope that connected us together.

'Mick!' I shouted down so he could hear.

'What, Pen? I'm slightly busy down here,' he replied, in his usual understated style.

'Mate, can you hold on a minute? I need to make a phone call,' I yelled in reply.

And so Mick balanced roughly 600 feet above the ground while I took care of charity business on what I had told Louise was meant to be a week off.

But whilst Louise was a complete pain in my backside at times, she was also the reason that we could do what we did. We needed a more than reliable person on the ground in Afghanistan managing the day-to-day care of the animals; to manage both sides of the charity, I had to be based in England, travelling out to Afghanistan when I could or heading off in the completely opposite direction, to America, to fundraise and draw in supporters.

Louise got the job done. Her list of contacts was extensive across Afghanistan and nearly all seemed to owe her a favour or two. Which was a good thing, because we had to call them in regularly.

When Danielle had come to the decision that Wylie would not survive much longer roaming on the airfield base as he did – his limited sense of survival badly letting him down time and time again – she had, when pressed, reluctantly handed over responsibility for Wylie to our Nowzad Dogs charity.

And so we had taken on the mission to get him safely from Kandahar to Kabul.

chapter 14

Night Time Manoeuvres

The phone vibrated again, the illumination from the small screen not really making a dent in the pitch-black of the room.

I had ignored the phone once already, furiously hoping it was a wrong number. Only yesterday it would have been Louise's Afghan mobile ringing in the room next door instead of mine, and I could have just rolled over to sleep again, smug in the knowledge she would deal with whatever the emergency was that demanded a call in the middle of the night.

But Louise was well on her way to England by now, so when it rang for the second time in quick succession, I had no choice but to answer it.

The darkness of the room didn't help as I sat up and reluctantly attempted to get my bearings. I reached for the annoying source of the buzzing and pressed the button to accept the call, holding the phone to my ear.

'Hey, Marnie, how are you?' I asked as enthusiastically as I could for two-thirty in the morning, knowing full well that by the end of the call I would be getting dressed and heading out for an early morning stroll.

'Pen, the dogs are barking,' Marnie stated simply.

'Yup, already dressed and about to check it out,' I lied. I had heard them barking but had kept my eyes closed and tried to wait it out. Hoping the bloody lot of them would pack it in and settle down without the need for me to leave the comfort of my bed.

I had only been in Kabul for three days and already I was sleep deprived.

'OK, thanks Pen.' *Click*. The connection was cut.

The Royal Marines had spent a lot of time preparing me to stay alive in shit-has-hit-the-fan moments. I was well aware this was not one of those moments, but it did absolutely no harm to remember the lessons as, after all, I was in Afghanistan, only this time without a gun of my own nor several highly trained armed men just around the corner. The key to working in Afghanistan was not to become complacent.

Every night, when finally I got on top of the workload and my bed beckoned, I would without fail pack everything I might need should I have to get out of Dodge quickly: passport, money, laptop and basic war-zone first-aid items, all in my grab bag hanging by the door, my clothes laid out ready to throw on if I was forced to make an escape.

Running away naked was not on my agenda.

I rolled out of bed and more or less fell into my pre-placed clothes, on the chair exactly one arm-span from the left side of the bed. Before I had even reached the light switch by the door I was dressed, my head torch in my pocket for the dark but fairly short walk to the Nowzad animal shelter so that I could deal with the source that had caused the barking frenzy: Wylie.

The bloody mutt had only been here two weeks and was already number one on the shelter's trouble-maker list.

Louise had warned me this would happen. I just had not believed her.

When I had started the charity in May 2007, we had piggy-backed the soldiers' dog rescues that we had been asked to assist with on the back of a small dog rescue operation run by an American journalist called Pam who rented a family compound which had first taken in my dog, Nowzad, during my hour of need, but we had very quickly outgrown that cramped compound in the middle of Kabul: within days of having a web presence, we had been inundated with messages from soldiers from America, Canada, the United Kingdom, Holland and South Africa all serving in Afghanistan and all desperate for their new four-legged buddy to be 'rescued' to their family home.

The compound had been able to hold maybe twenty dogs at a push, and that had meant them being crammed three or four to a run that was originally designed for only one dog.

Assessing the potential for future demand, we had reckoned that we would need space for at least fifty or more dogs. And with that had come the noise associated with fifty dogs to contend with.

Dogs, especially feral ones, don't keep their displeasure concerning the nearness of other dogs to themselves. Being located in an over-populated area of Kabul meant the noise of barking dogs was an issue.

Our charity had grand plans and needed substantial grounds of its own. But where? Kabul was a densely popu-lated city of some 3.7 million. There were not that many spots you could plonk a dog shelter on and assume everybody would be happy. After all, the random barking from the countless strays living on Kabul's dusty, rubbish-strewn streets was already a universal Afghan complaint. I didn't think it would go down too well with any potential neighbours if we began building a shelter with the intention of actually housing dogs in their neighbourhood.

Options for land on which to build a shelter were few and far between. And bloody expensive. The American war machine had thrown money at Afghanistan, creating a major artificial housing and land bubble. Instead of bartering and paying local rents, the money men had basically signed blank cheques to ensure a swift and easy deal for the housing and land required to support the war effort. I had been disgusted by the blatant waste of western money. And even more horrified when I had discovered that even on the outskirts of Kabul, we were looking at $150,000 for just two acres of dirt.

'Seriously?' I had stated repeatedly to the Afghan landowner, as I had explained hysterically that my own house in the UK didn't bloody cost that much.

It was a concept he couldn't understand. The Americans were rich, so it followed that we were too.

But another American, originally from the city of coffee and grunge – Seattle – had saved the day. With curling dark hair that sat on top of her shoulders, unless covered with a head scarf, and soft, kind eyes, Marnie surprised Afghans and westerners alike with her mastery of the Dari language and no-nonsense approach.

We often chatted about the old Afghanistan she had known over a cup of her favourite coffee, while I drank English tea, in her family kitchen in Kabul. Growing up in Kabul as a teenager, she had experienced the innocence of a country happy with its moderate Islam and acceptance of other cultures; a country that could not imagine the horrors the next forty years were about to bring. Back then, it had not been out of the ordinary to see American, teenaged girls riding to school along the streets of Kabul wearing a pair of shorts.

I knew it would be a very short-lived outing if any western woman were to consider that 'risk' attire these days.

Marnie and her family had been stayed in Kabul from '64 to '69 and had been sad to leave a country that was so more accommodating than the country of today. She had always known, however, that she would return at some point. She had just had no idea of the drastic changes Afghanistan would undergo.

Marnie came back in 2004 along with her husband, Norm, a charming, softly spoken American. Both of them worked for the non-governmental organisation known simply as PARSA, the full title of Physiotherapy and Rehabilitation Services for Afghanistan proving too much of a mouthful for most. An organisation that worked directly to improve the lives of the disadvantaged communities in Afghanistan, Dr Norm, as he was affectionately known by the PARSA staff, would quietly work behind the scenes whilst Marnie strode out in front along with Yasin, her Afghan PARSA director.

More comfortable in western clothes than traditional Afghan attire, Yasin was a passionate and very confident character, fluent in English and determined to make a difference for his fellow countrymen who had not been given the same opportunities as him.

The previous summer during 2010, I had flown via an aid flight to Bamyan Province, situated in the Hindu Kush mountains of central Afghanistan with Yasin, the equivalent road journey a far more dangerous proposition for a westerner than the seriously old Soviet helicopter tasked for the journey, even if the tattered flight safety card only in Russian had not instilled confidence in either of us. But it was a damn bit quicker than the bus: hours rather than days. We had stayed at a PARSA-run guest house located just off the main street in what was downtown Bamiyan City. The bustle of the busy market street was kept at bay by the high mud walls surrounding the traditionally basic Afghan compound. The house had been simply decorated and bare of luxuries, but we had feasted like royalty on a banquet of Afghan food prepared by a cook over a single gas ring, served on an intricately painted wooden table that was suitably low to the ground to ensure we sat on the carpeted floor to eat. I had slept outside on the porch in a vain attempt to keep cool, kept company by the resident family's dog, until the early morning call of the compound cockerel had roused us both. Yasin had relished the opportunity to show me rural Afghanistan. His Afghanistan. And I enjoyed his company. He was as passionate about dogs as Marnie was, owning several himself.

PARSA had been operating in Afghanistan since 1996, even operating secret schools during the dark days of Taliban rule, the brainchild of a remarkable woman called Mary MacMakin. Mary, a physical therapist, had already worked extensively in Afghanistan for many, many years but had become frustrated with the lack of facilities for the desperately ignored widowed women, left to fend for themselves on the streets of Kabul. She knew she had to do something to make a difference. Her solution to try and turn the tide and provide support to the widows, disabled and orphans of Afghanistan had led to the formation of PARSA.

Marnie had taken on the role of PARSA's executive director and, along with Yasin, they attempted to guide and steer the NGO through the course of the turbulent years of transition from Taliban neglect to the coalition's efforts to bring stability and democracy to the people of Afghanistan. And both were doing a damn fine job.

Set in beautiful orchards surrounded by arable land, PARSA was a hidden jewel in the fume-choked city of Kabul. Marnie and Norm lived in the rambling, one-storey flat-roofed house which, the story went, was formerly a residence of the Taliban. The house reminded me of the inside of Dr Who's Tardis, the many rooms all interconnected via several internal doors that meant you really never needed to leave the same way you entered. I had discovered seven different entry points to arrive in the kitchen alone. It meant that a mobile phone was essential to locate Marnie if she wasn't at the kitchen table glued to her laptop and a million PARSA emails, as searching the many rooms was a very time-consuming exercise. We had all shared the frustration of rushing into the kitchen after being summoned by Marnie for a meeting only to find her chair empty. But then often, a swift call to her mobile would reveal her forgotten phone vibrating away on the brightly decorated table cloth, next to a half-drunk mug of coffee.

'Marnnnieeee!'

Plush Afghan rugs hung from the walls, beautifully carved traditional wooden furniture complemented every room and the tall, whitewashed ceilings kept the house relatively cool in the desperately hot summers but numbingly cold in the winter. Then, the winter wood burners greedily depleted the wood pile to keep the rooms at even a bearable temperature.

But the enormous walled garden had offered Marnie the opportunity to indulge her second passion in life: Afghan street dogs; Norm reluctantly accepting that he hadn't made Marnie's top two, and that Afghanistan and dogs came first.

Marnie had wanted to implement an animal welfare programme to make a difference for the street dogs of Kabul, but was limited by the scope of PARSA's remit in Afghanistan. Even with Yasin's fondness for dogs and backing for such a programme, both were unable to proceed. In Afghanistan, you don't mix animal welfare with the welfare of children. It is just not a socially accepted norm. And so Marnie had had to restrict herself to rescuing only the occasional stray in need.

Much to the dismay of Norm, however, the promise of keeping the rescued dogs in their house down to single figures was abandoned all too soon, but the novelty of the night-time 'dogstacle' course to answer a call of nature had soon worn off when the aptly named Rambo, a young German shepherd cross pup, had begun to make his displeasure fiercely known when woken from a deep sleep at his regular spot curled next to the toilet.

His overly enthusiastic barking could often be misconstrued as aggressive, but even though he was just scared and unsure of himself, his throaty *yap yap* would echo around the rooms and hallways of the darkened house, signalling the wake-up call for the many other settled rescues who had been sleeping peacefully in various corners of the formerly silent building. Now all fully alert and happy to join the early morning chorus.

Marnie had needed somebody with her single-mindedness to succeed to manage an animal welfare programme for Kabul, and joining forces with Nowzad Dogs had satisfied both our desires to do something positive for the dogs of Kabul.

Offering our charity the opportunity to rent a parcel of land on the PARSA property had been a lifeline we had very much needed to grab. The icing on the cake, too, was when Marnie, without hesitation, opened the spare rooms in their house for us to take over and use as a clinic, cattery and staff rooms.

Marnie had given the Nowzad Dogs charity its first proper footing in Afghanistan.

With my trips to Afghanistan few and far between, the charity still young and needing to be guided and developed as it grew a supporter base in the United Kingdom – and, much to my surprise, the rest of the world – I had concluded that I needed somebody in-country full time to manage the Afghan staff we now out of necessity had to employ to feed and clean out the dogs at our shelter on Marnie's land, and ensure the two vets we had taken on actually did know what they said they knew.

Thus Louise had been a god-send.

As I jogged steadily down the pitch-black, tree-lined road towards the shelter, the beam from my head torch illuminating the five yards of tarmac directly in front of me, the noise of frenziedly barking dogs was actually pretty loud.

I reached the metal gates and fumbled with the padlock so I could get inside, the dogs increasing their rowdy barking and howling at the sound of my arrival.

As I hastily opened the gate and slipped in as quickly as I could, swiftly closing the gate behind me, a fluffy shadow of darkness ran though the beam of my torch and back into the blackness and wall of deafening barking.

'Wylie!' I shouted to be heard. The little git had again – we had yet to figure out how – climbed over the chain-link fencing of his run to get into the buffer area of land that led to the main entrance to the shelter.

'Get your arse over here now,' I demanded.

He knew the drill. I was sure he did this just to get me to come along and say hello to him in the middle of the night.

Wylie scampered back into the beam of my torch and promptly sat on his haunches, head cocked to one side, piercing orange eyes reflecting the torch light.

'Nice one, mate.' I reached into my pocket. 'Any chance we can go back to bed, please?' I asked.

Wylie gently nibbled the biscuit and then turned to walk back towards his vacated run. I followed him, yelling at our other canine residents to shut up. Without any further hassle, I let Wylie back into his run and Eidy, a white and brown patched dog with two fast-growing pups, rushed over to check her kennel mate had returned safe from his night-time manoeuvres.

'Eidy, next time, stop him will you, please?' I pushed a biscuit through the chain link for her. I had a soft spot for Eidy.

As I walked back to the house and my bed, I chuckled to myself in the dark. Without the head torch turned on, the moonlight bathed everything in an eerie, silvery light which, as my eyes became accustomed to the lack of artificial light, provided more than enough ambient light to see clearly by. The stars above Kabul were always gloriously bright.

Managing the shelter daily was exhausting in itself, let alone all the out of hours issues that cropped up and had to be dealt with. I still couldn't believe we had found someone willing to live and work in Kabul more or less full-time, without many complaints.

I really did hope Louise was enjoying her time off at home, although the continuous emails I was receiving from her told me that she was still very much plugged into Nowzad daily life. When she came back to Afghan, though, we had a serious amount of work to do figuring out how to keep the noise from the dogs to bearable levels, as there had been talk that we would need to leave the safe haven that Marnie had provided. I had hoped that the rumours were just trying to scare us into keeping the noise levels down, as I couldn't see how we could communicate this need to the dogs. Dogs living in packs barked. And that was part of life.

chapter 15

Shelter Life

'OK, Wylie.' I stared into his tiger-like orangey brown eyes. 'We need to come to some kind of agreement here, buddy, because this just isn't funny anymore.' I wiped the sweat from my eyes.

The chase had been short-lived, but it was still more than enough physical exertion to bring an instant sweat on in the zapping heat of the afternoon.

Wylie, I hazarded a guess, thought it was actually quite amusing: his quarter-length tail just waved at me casually as he lay in a plough-furrow of the field, little wafts of dust kicking up as it brushed lightly across the cracked mud each time.

The little bugger was probably enjoying the attention.

Wylie reminded me of Steve McQueen and the legendary film *The Great Escape*. Mr McQueen, cast as Captain Virgil Hilts, aka 'the Cooler King', was throughout the film always testing and pushing at the Germans with his escape attempts. Each time he was caught, he remained calm and relaxed about being returned to the prison camp and a stint in the cooler. The only difference between Virgil and Wylie was that there was no time-out cooler waiting for the wayward dog's return, but a bowl of what we called 'dog soup'.

Buying standard dry dog food was a non-starter in Kabul so Louise had improvised: potatoes, carrots, rice, naan bread and maybe some chicken were all mixed together in an enormous cooking pot that our staff stirred to perfection each day. It actually didn't taste too bad, although the staff had declined my offer to try some the first time we'd made it. Holding their heads in their hands as I had munched away on a spoonful of the gruel-like mixture, I had quickly realised I probably wouldn't particularly fancy it every day.

As I knelt with McQueen dog, I realised we were a good 300 yards out from the shelter gates, in the open expanse of arable land that PARSA had designated for the growing of alfalfa, a flowering plant that is used as an important forage crop in many countries around the world, especially Afghanistan. Widowed women, normally outcast from society and unable to secure honest and, more to the point, safe work, tended the fields as part of the PARSA community programme that taught them skills vital to the Afghan village way of life especially if they did not have a man of the household who would normally have taken responsibility for those tasks.

Looking at him there in the dust, I suddenly groaned. The dog that would just never give up his escape attempts had presented me with a dilemma: in my rush to pursue Wylie, I had forgotten to grab a dog lead.

I would have to carry Wylie back – he was too short in the legs for me to hold by the scruff of the neck and walk back together side by side without me having to crouch over like the Hunchback of Notre Dame, an ordeal my back would not enjoy at all.

There was nothing else for it. I scooped up the relaxed fluffball into the crook of my arms and then heaved him over my shoulder as a fireman would when rescuing a damsel in distress from a burning building.

Except this damsel was a guy with questionable breath, covered in dust and probably crawling with just a few ticks and fleas.

'Let's go, Steve.'

Wylie made no attempt to wriggle free as he rode high on my shoulder, facing back the way we had come, no doubt savouring the brief moments of freedom he had had as he had thrashed his way through the grassy field. And, just like the POWs in *The Great Escape* cheering and welcoming Steve McQueen's character back once again, as we entered through the large shelter gates, the barking of all the other shelter residents reached a crescendo as his canine compatriots cheered his return.

'Your fans welcome you back, Wylie,' I shouted to him to be heard over the ruckus.

I guess I couldn't blame Wylie for wanting to be free. This was a dog that until now had been as free as a bird, more or less able to wander at will and choose his own surroundings. There was no way I could explain to this wayward mutt that his current period of captivity, which included being fed a decent meal each day, was in his best interests as we continued to push the fundraising efforts and waited for him to finish his course of vaccinations for export.

Louise had phoned me on the first day of Wylie's arrival at the shelter to tell me that he was fairly nifty at vacating his run at will.

She had pulled out all the stops to have Wylie transported by air to Kabul – there was no way we could trust an Afghan driver to keep him secure and safe in the back of an Afghan taxi for the long journey north from Kandahar, the preferred method of bringing rescued dogs or cats to our shelter. We had seen it all: puppies jammed in between luggage in the boot of a car; one small dog smuggled inside a combat jacket while the owner took a military helicopter flight to Kabul on a pretend errand; and, recently, two young cats sent from Herat in an unmarked wooden box that I had eventually found making its third revolution of the baggage carousel at Kabul International Airport. How the unaccompanied box had even made the flight we had no idea, but the cats had made it safely so we chalked it up as a success!

Louise had known she could not trust a driver to keep tabs on Wylie: one slightest error in leaving a door open too long and Wylie would never have been seen again. So she had called in a favour. The Central Asia Development Group, CADG for short, specialised in operating in remote areas of Central Asia and the Middle East, which among their many areas of expertise included logistics and aviation. They flew occasionally from Kandahar to Kabul, and the pilots were sympathetic to the plight of the strays adopted by soldiers and our role in supporting those rescue attempts.

Danielle had been tasked with delivering Wylie to the flight line at the preordained time in a homemade travel crate knocked up by the soldiers at the checkpoint, designed to keep Wylie safely contained for the hop up to Kabul. Images of Wylie strolling up and down the cabin of the twin-engine light aircraft had been very much in everybody's mind.

Incredibly, the many working parts to the mission had gelled together seamlessly, thanks to the thorough prior planning of Louise which had enabled our driver, Wahidullah, to collect the now former resident of Kandahar's streets without a hitch.

But it had been a close call for Wylie in the preceding days before his planned flight. Yet again, much to the horror of all who had become close to the lovable rogue, he had demonstrated his unnerving ability to be in the wrong place at the wrong time. Casually lying out in the sun, at the entrance to entry checkpoint five, Wylie had been coaxed over to a group of local Afghan men, who had tempted him to leave the security of the checkpoint with offerings of food.

It had been a ploy to get their hands on one of the dogs that they had witnessed receiving the lavish affection of the white woman soldier during the animal clinics. They could not for one minute understand why, but they knew the dog had meaning for the soldiers at the checkpoint.

Being unable to directly assault the coalition soldiers without mounting a full-scale attack, they chose the cowardly option instead of targeting Wylie, knowing full well that he was very much a positive aspect of checkpoint life. Maiming the dog would most definitely cause the soldiers pain, as the men knew full well that the rules of engagement that all coalition troops were ordered to follow forbade them becoming involved in an attack on a feral dog.

Much to the vile delight of his tormentors, the soldiers would be forced to just stand and watch.

Indeed, the soldiers had watched aghast, and completely unable to act, as Wylie had suddenly been thrown into the path of an oncoming SUV truck.

Bouncing off the grill, the dog had disappeared under the vehicle. The driver, clearly determined not to become involved in what he assumed could escalate into a nasty encounter between the hate-filled locals and the now angry soldiers, had chosen to accelerate off along the road. In his wake, a crumpled and once-more battered Wylie lay stunned on the tarmac surface.

Gathering a hastily formed patrol together, ensuring that their exposed flanks were being covered by other soldiers in the adjacent guard towers, the troops rushed out to recover Wylie back to the safety of the checkpoint.

Once more, Danielle received the dreaded call that Wylie had been in the wars again. Fearing the worst when she heard that he had actually been hit by a car, she had gathered her medical supplies and rushed over to the checkpoint to treat him. Had he been injured too badly this time?

Wylie was obviously made of unbreakable stuff as he was on his feet by the time she got there to tend to him, his short, fluffy tail greeting her as he recognised his best pal. Danielle crouched down to hug the once-again lucky dog. But she was surely counting down the days until she could put Wylie on the flight to the Nowzad shelter.

And it had seemed that Australian rescues were like waiting for a bus – none had trundled up the road but then suddenly, out of nowhere, two came along together. Within days of us receiving Wylie into the safety of the shelter, we were contacted by a young Australian rifleman named Nathan.

Located out in the remote Mirabad Valley near the multinational base at Tarin Kowt, the soldier had been patrolling and searching *quala*s – Afghan farm compounds. Entering one *quala*, he had immediately noticed a frightened tan and white pup, ears cropped close to the sides of his head, chained up in the corner of the compound.

At the sounds of the soldiers searching the farm, the pup had begun barking and jumping in anticipation of further human company. The Afghan children's solution to prevent his barking had been to kick the dog in the head.

When Nathan, appalled, had stepped in to prevent further abuse, the dog had instantly squatted and peed in frightened submission as he approached.

Using his translator to question the farm owner, it was understood that the dog was to be used as a fighting dog during the upcoming tournaments held in nearby Tarin Kowt. As he had listened to the conversation, Nathan had crouched down to stroke the pup, figuring it to be around five months old. It was definitely a Kuchi, its large paws signs of the big lad he would become. Nathan had spoken softly to the pup, attempting to reassure it that it wouldn't be harmed. Its thick leather collar was tied on far too tightly, and dug painfully into the distressed dog's neck.

It was a simple decision to make. The Australian soldiers bartered with the pup's owner, coming to agree a $300 fee for it to be handed over to the infantrymen.

The patrol had continued its route back towards the security of their base along a tree-lined, unplanted field, except that this time the patrol had gained a member. Nathan, his rifle hanging downwards in his right hand, carried the pup unceremoniously with his left hand tucked under its belly, slightly propping its weight on the top of his chest-rig ammunition pouches as he walked. The pup, although unsure of what was happening, just dangled there, riding against his rescuer's combat jacket.

Nathan pondered how he was going to bring up the fact to his other half that he was coming home from Afghan with a new buddy in tow. He knew he would have to tell her about his impulsive decision as soon as he could find a free time slot to use the sat phone.

Behind him, the patrol interpreter smiled broadly as Nathan's oppo turned around to take a quick photo of the strange patrolling technique. The 'terp' just thought to himself how strange the westerners were as he continued to follow the big Australian soldier carrying the pup.

When I had replied to Nathan stating that the Nowzad Dogs charity was of course able to support his request to take on the pup he had now named 'AJ', I had asked if his family was aware and willing to take on what was going to be a fairly big dog.

A simple but to-the-point reply had appeared in my inbox: 'I have cleared it with the missus.' I had smiled. That was good enough for me.

And so here we were, standing outside the amateur-built run, five of us huddled in a group, the majority Afghan, debating Wylie's escape techniques and how we intended to keep him inside his run. My broken Farsi, the main language spoken in the north of the country which was much softer than the guttural sounding Pashtun of the south and the staff's non-existent English was, strangely enough, no barrier to the heated debate and subsequent plan of action.

How Wylie had escaped again none of us could under-stand. The chain-link fence was five feet high around his run, and then there was the outer shelter fence he had scaled as well, just for good measure. Somehow Spider Dog had climbed both in his attempt to vacate the shelter. For the life of me, I could not figure out how he could balance delicately enough on the top of a piece of chain-link fence without slip-ping a paw through the many gaps, before hanging himself upside down. He was either very lucky or had the balance of a ninja.

Taking into account his previous escapades, I came down on the side of lucky *and* being a ninja.

I turned my head sideways to look across at a run two doors down, and the fast-growing pup that was AJ. Flat on his side, fast asleep, there had been not one escape attempt. Not even once.

I shook my head as I looked back towards Wylie. 'AJ knows when he has it good. Why can't you?' Wylie just stared back at me, pink tongue hanging out his mouth as he tried to keep cool in the heat.

Either way, we spent the rest of the afternoon toiling in the almost unbearable heat to attach a further piece of chain-link fencing to the top of his run, hanging it at a slight inwards incline in a vain attempt to put him off his climb.

Wylie sat inside his run, eyeing our work with interest. 'That should keep you in,' I stated matter of factly. 'No more great escapes!'

The look on Wylie's face should really have told me all I needed to know.

chapter 16

Wyliiieeeeee

'Wyliiiieeeeeeeeeee!' I screamed frantically, in between sucking in desperately needed lungfuls of hot, dusty air.

The mid afternoon sun, beating down relentlessly, had boiled the mercury to a sweat-inducing plus 40°C. It was no time to be sprinting like a loon across an empty field. My shirt was already soaked with sweat. The annoying fact that it was only clean on that morning flashed through my brain as I continued the chase.

'Bloody dog,' I cursed out loud as I anticipated the lengthy jump across the drainage ditch that dissected the ploughed field. With luck on my side, although hitting the opposite bank hard, I just managed to keep my stride going forward.

Wylie, the athletic bugger, had cleared the gap easily. Just like he had somehow managed to clear the top of the shelter fencing once more just a few minutes earlier. I was just relieved I had been in the vicinity to actually see him making his dash for freedom.

In full sprint mode, arms pumping vigorously by my sides as I tried to improve my pace, I suddenly realised the northern end of the field was approaching rapidly. Bad news.

Picking up my pace once again, I glimpsed a quarter-length bushy tail whooshing through the tall, tinder-dry grass that formed a natural buffer between the field and the track.

The track ran the full length of this side of the field and served as a shortcut for the locals between their place of work at PARSA and where they lived nearby. I caught sight of the escapee again as he sped along the track, now joined by a mud wall that marked the boundary of a family compound that backed on to the field.

Between watching my footing and scouting ahead to keep tabs on Wylie's progress, I managed to shortcut the distance to the track, bursting out of the field closer to the fleeing hound.

'Damn it!'

Wylie had switched right and I watched his tail disappear after his body around the corner of the wall that now turned back towards the front of the family house.

I threw my right hand out to act as a pivot point, catching the corner of the rough textured wall, dry mud flaking away as I swung myself around the wall after the Houdini dog.

Feeling the exertion taking its toll, I made a mental note to maybe work a bit harder during my evening exercise hour, round the back of the clinic – my improvised outdoor gym testimony to the fact that I couldn't totally shake my past as a Royal Marine.

Still running, I realised my trouser pocket had relieved itself of the burden of my mobile phone as I increased the pace. Stopping to retrieve it was not an option at this point; collecting it would have to wait. 'I cannot lose this dog!' I screamed at myself as I focused on his gazelle-like sprint to freedom. For a dog with short legs he was bloody fast.

Wylie was galloping along in front of me, parallel to the centuries-old wall, just fifty feet ahead. I wasn't closing the gap. I kept forgetting I was forty-two these days and not the twenty-five years young I liked to think I still was. But I had to catch him – as soon as the dog with the out-of-control hair rounded the next corner then it was open ground and game over. The sparsely vegetated estate that backed on to the clinic was vast, and finding him would be like searching for the proverbial needle in a haystack.

Just before the northern end of the plateau, where it began to climb sharply upwards in the steep contours of the jagged mountain standing guard over us, sat a large, modern, two-storey school building and three blocks of Soviet-built flats that now housed a widowed women's refuge. After that, if he chose not to run up the mountain, then to the west and east lay the sprawling mass of the third fastest-growing city in the world, a fume-filled collection of hustle and bustle, bartering and trading, with everybody trying to earn a living however they could. Most definitely not a place for a dog that loved being around people who mostly didn't want dogs near them.

Of course, Wylie high-tailed it round the last corner. That was it. There were too many open directions he could take.

'I'm going to lose him.'

As I flung myself around the corner after him, sweat pouring off me, I stopped dead in my tracks. Doubled over, hands on my knees as I sucked in lungful after lungful of much needed O_2, I dropped into a crouch, one hand propping me upright on the rock-hard mud track as I managed a smile towards the reason I had abandoned the chase.

Maybe thirty feet in front of me, squatting as all Afghan men seemed able to do for hours upon end, was a grinning figure, his back against the smooth compound wall, shaded from the glaring rays of the rising morning sun.

And, sitting quite relaxed between his legs, panting slightly, was Mr Houdini dog: Wylie, his golden eyes wide-open, staring intently at me as he enjoyed the attention Wassah was giving him.

'You bugger!' I spluttered, for Wylie's benefit.

Wearing his trademark light grey cargo trousers and blue short-sleeved T-shirt, Wassah, his shoulder-length jet-black hair and gringo moustache making him a spit of the bass player from the rock band, Spinal Tap, was my now widely grinning saviour.

Wassah was employed by Marnie and worked as a kind of general fix-it man for the many repairs needed to maintain the crumbling house, whilst also taking care of her ever-expanding dog rescue population.

He had obviously just snuck out for a sneaky cigarette, as the telltale butt lay smoking slightly on the ground to the left of his American-issue combat boots.

'Pen, Pen,' he said, laughing softly as he carefully patted Wylie on the head. The wayward dog just tipped his head back further, demanding more attention. Wassah was very good with dogs.

Wassah's funky seventies look hid a past not envied or rivalled by many. In the days of the Afghan civil war he had sided with the Northern Alliance under the leadership of Massoud as they continually repelled the Taliban's attempt to claim the north of the country, thereby preventing the complete control of all of Afghanistan. He had been captured and spent time idling in a harsh Taliban jail which, naturally enough, had only reinforced his resolve to continue the fight against the Talibs.

Walking past one day, pretty soon after we had located to Marnie's house, he had found me sitting at the kitchen table sending emails. I had closed down the email program just as Wassah looked over and he had noticed my laptop screen-saver: a group of heavily armed Marines faced the camera for a post-battle photograph, each posing casually as if our first battle had been just a run-of-the-mill outing. The background scenery of desert and sandbagged positions clearly placed the photograph as having been taken somewhere in Afghanistan. All of us were decked out in our combat body armour, tooled up with weapons and grenades. In fact, it had been anything but run of the mill with the Taliban hitting us from behind as we had left a dam complex in the town of Gereshk.

Wassah had grabbed me by the shoulder and said 'Helmand?', looking at me with surprise.

Up until then, I had figured he had assumed I was just a crazy dog person from the west with nothing better to do than travel to war-torn Kabul preaching animal welfare.

'Afghanistan,' I replied, nodding my head. 'Marine.' I tapped myself proudly on the chest and then pointed to the smiling, good-looking sergeant standing amongst the young and now not so rookie lads of Five Troop, Kilo Company, 42 Commando Royal Marines.

Wassah had given me a thumbs-up with his right hand and slapped me hard on the back. Very hard.

I had long ago learnt that Afghans never used their left hand to indicate anything. Its sole function in life was related to an activity that was never a subject for public discussion, unlike the weird British obsession with it. To fully under-stand the issue, one would only have to bear in mind that for most of the population, finding toilet paper is a novelty in Afghanistan. When I signed for receipts or wrote out a shop-ping list in front of the staff, I would look up knowingly to answer their silent stares: 'Yes, I am left handed.' They always appeared surprised and disgusted at the same time. It just was not the 'done' thing out there. They had never met anyone left handed before.

Nodding his head slowly in appreciation, his hair ludicrously longer than any other Afghan man's hair I had seen, Wassah continued staring at my screensaver and simply said, '*Khub*.' He had said, 'Good.'

Praise like that from a Northern Alliance enemy of the Taliban was praise enough in my book.

Figuring his mental image of me had now changed, I hoped I was now vaguely in his league. I had stood up and nodded to agree, extending my right hand to say thank you. But Wassah had lunged forward and grabbed me in a vice-like bear hug as he had shaken me up and down, laughing the whole time as I was easily thrown around like a rag doll.

'OK, OK, mate,' I pleaded as his arms squeezed me painfully.

Wassah had finally placed me back on the floor and we had smiled at each other as he had taken one last look at the photo. He had then indicated for me to follow him as he bounded from the kitchen.

I guessed at once where we were going. The clock on the kitchen wall told me it was staff lunch time.

I am not the most adventurous of food folk. Beige food is my favourite and only kind of food, meaning simply no greens and not a lot of reds and most definitely no exotic fruits – Granny Smiths will do me just fine. The Afghan-prepared meal that I had eaten back in the day with the Helmand police during our tour of duty, all of us sitting crossed-legged on a carpeted floor in a plainly decorated room, eating rice with our fingers, had probably been the highlight of my culinary craziness. My unadventurous food streak was regularly a talking point when I went out to eat with Hannah especially when she ordered dishes that consisted of food stuffs that I regarded as completely inedible.

It was clear that Wassah was on a mission to reveal my former Afghan past to the Nowzad staff, and he hurriedly led the way to the current staff eating area which, in the 40° heat of the midday sun, had been located in the gloriously cool shade of a grand old tree, its big-leafed branches forming a natural sun canopy for us to shelter under.

Our staff chef, Zakia, had already been busy serving plates of cooked food she had prepared earlier; our daily shelter staff: Safi, Zahir and Kahn, all still decked out in coveralls grubby from the kennel cleaning tasks; along with Wahidullah, our driver; and our head vet, Dr Hadi, were sitting cross-legged on the dusty, red-patterned carpet in anticipation of the lunch to come, their shoes neatly placed in a row at the ragged edge of the carpet.

Before I had even had time to unlace my boots, Wassah had been speed-talking in Dari and enthusiastically gesturing in my direction, while the other staff laughed and clapped their approval.

I had an idea what he was saying, but didn't begin to understand the detail. Frankly, I was amazed that he had that much to say just from seeing just one photo. So I played along and pretended I was holding a rifle. This spurred them on to even more jubilant applause.

As the hubbub died down I thanked them, and continued removing my well-worn desert combat boots. I had always known that keeping what had proved to be an extremely comfortable pair of boots when I handed back the majority of my military gear to the regimental quartermaster when I was medically discharged from the Royal Marines would one day be of benefit. Those boots now served me well once more in Afghanistan but, due to the lacing system, were a bugger to take off. But I was fully aware of the Afghan custom that dictated that you always removed footwear when entering the home or, in this case, sitting on a carpet laid outside on the rock-hard, sun-scorched ground for lunch, so I persevered.

Dr Hadi and Wahidullah had shuffled sideways to create a gap to allow me space to sit between them. I made the best attempt I could at sitting cross-legged.

'Damn,' I squeaked as I tried, without success, to feel comfortable for more than a few seconds. Barring the few meals I'd had with the Afghan police force, primary school had been the last time I had happily sat like this, I realised.

I had looked sideways at a grinning Wahidullah, easily relaxed in the cross-legged position a billion people around this part of the world adopt as a matter of course.

'You fine, sir?' Wahidullah asked in English, as I had struggled once more to get my left knee to stay flat. It ended up more upright, and I had had to reposition my whole body once more to end up in an uncomfortable semi-crouch.

'*Bali*,' I replied. Lying that I was fine.

Zakia had already placed a bowl of today's lunch special in front of me. I felt proud that I recognised the rice and guessed the brownish, odd-shaped lumps were a meat of some kind, but the rest of it was a mystery.

A lot of it was beige, so maybe that was something in my favour?

Wahidullah was still watching me and had noticed my hesitancy at the plate of food placed in front of me.

'*Quorma chalaw.*' He pronounced the Afghan name for it proudly before pointing to each item in turn and speaking in his broken English: 'Meat, bean, onion, eggplant, rice,' as he scooped up a mouthful from his own plate, obviously using his right hand.

The 'beans' looked like no beans I had ever seen before. And I knew that eggs didn't grow on plants, so a surprise definitely awaited my tastebuds. At least using my right hand was now second nature in Kabul. I was well trained.

'No problem, I can do this,' I reassured myself as I tucked in.

The sloppy mixture actually didn't taste too bad. The fact that everybody was staring at me was slightly off-putting, though. I had just hoped Zakia had really cooked and washed everything properly. My stomach, without fail, always took a few days to get used to Afghan hygiene.

The conversation had flowed around the carpet, mainly in Dari, with Dr Hadi translating anything aimed in my direction. I had continued to go through the motions of scooping up a few more mouthfuls, mainly of rice if I could help it, as I had nodded happily and tried to join in the conversation.

Dr Hadi had then passed me a side dish of sorts, which consisted of several large green leaves and one thin, curly chilli pepper, native to Afghanistan and not for the faint hearted, I had been told previously.

I should never have looked up, but I did. Wassah was staring at me intently as he slowly chewed one of the peppers. He seemed to be savouring it as his eyes never left mine.

Right at that moment, I had known that the next few minutes were not going to end well for me.

Smiling, Wassah had nodded intently towards the single stranded pepper lying on the plate in front of me. The smile seemed to me to contain just a hint of menace. After all, this man had spent time in a Taliban jail and relished it. And he had just challenged me.

I noticed the conversation around the carpet had died. 'Oh, crap.'

I took one look around the faces on the carpet – all had been weighing up my next move. All wearing a stupid grin. Knowing what I didn't know.

For me, I realised with dismay, it was time to back up the photo image of a hardened Marine.

'Bastard,' was all I could think.

As I had reached forward to pick up the green monster from the plate, its slimy olive-shiny sides silently goading me to eat it, the staff had begun to clap. Zahir being the most enthusiastic had whooped and hollered as I held the chilli pepper aloft, close to my mouth.

'For queen and country,' I had said smartly, for no one's benefit but my own as a delaying tactic, before I placed the whole thing in my mouth and started to chew, never letting my eyes stray from Wassah and his ever-widening grin.

I don't think he had expected me to eat the whole thing at once.

'It's not too bad,' I spluttered as I crunched the pepper's outer shell. There was a lot of chilli pepper in my mouth and, as I chewed rapidly, I had attempted to swallow as much as I could. 'Get it down the hatch,' I thought to myself. 'Job done.'

I guess they knew something was wrong when my face started to scrunch up. I knew something was wrong when the slight burning sensation started to grow at the back of my throat.

Sure, I had figured there would be some sort of uncomfortable feeling but, within seconds, my mouth felt as if I was sucking on a burning mass of hot coals, and sweat had burst out of every pore on my face.

I was in trouble.

I threw my head around to the right and spat out every last piece of chilli pepper that I could, not caring if it landed on the carpet or not.

'Arrghhh, h-h-hot!' I shrieked as I turned back to the lunch setting and lunged for the water jug. I didn't bother with etiquette. I guzzled what was left straight from the jug as hysterical laughing echoed around the carpet.

Zakia was actually on her back from laughing so hard.

Gulping directly from the water jug had absolutely no effect on the furnace that was now where my mouth used to be. So I had jumped up and run the twenty feet to the water stand pipe that Wassah used to water the garden.

The howls of laughter had followed me.

My mouth was burning. It was unbearable. I ripped off the hose connection joint at the same time as I frantically turned on the tap. Water had burst out from the pipe in a thick torrent of fresh, cooling water straight from the deep well sunk on the property. I had just stuck my head under the flow and turned it with my mouth fully open, collecting the healing water, kneeling in a pool of muddy water as I tried desperately to cleanse the inside of my mouth.

I couldn't breathe but it felt good. The thought occurred to me that I was, in fact, using the now banned former CIA interrogation technique of 'water boarding' on myself. The joy.

My shirt had been soaked instantly and clung to my body, but I hadn't cared as I gasped for a quick breath before continuing the self-drowning exercise.

'Bastard,' was all I could say again as I had collapsed in a widening pool of water as the midday sun beat down.

Gales of laughter had continued to flow well into the afternoon.

As I now sat panting against the side of the wall, the chase over, I smiled across at Wassah as he continued to gently hold on to Wylie, the escape artist seemingly quite happy being sandwiched between the Afghan's legs.

As sweat poured down my face, I held an imaginary pepper to my lips.

Wassah whooped with laughter as he remembered the afternoon from many months before. He mimicked my action and held his own make-believe pepper aloft. 'Pen pepper,' he called over as he stood up with ease.

He had Wylie firmly by the scruff of the neck, ready to be taken back to the shelter. Wassah was a bit of a legend around these parts, and he had just saved my skin.

chapter 17

Ten Dollar Reward

I stank, big time.

It was only nine o'clock in the morning and I was dripping with sweat. My clean-on-that-morning shirt was
soaked through from my early morning exertions with
Wylie – the energy-sapping heat was already reaching the
mid-thirties.

I had remained sitting against the wall, regaining my breath
and hoping that I would stop sweating at some point as I
watched Wassah lead Wylie happily back to the kennels, his
short tail wagging away from side to side.

I seriously needed some water. I was gagging. But I
couldn't get up just at that moment, as my lungs were still
recovering from the unplanned Wylie exertions. With Kabul
sitting at around 1800m above sea level, any physical activity
always took a bit of getting used to. Especially when sprinting hell-for-leather across a ploughed field in a pair of combat
boots chasing a dog.

The relief at not losing Wylie was pretty immense.
Cheerfully, I figured if that was the worst the day had to offer,
then all was not so bad.

I stood up slowly, like an old man, and, still sweating, rounded the wall of Marnie's house and walked towards the open door of the clinic.

Our two clinic dogs, Buster and Foxy, ran parallel with me in their run.

'I'll come in and see you in a minute, guys,' I called over the chain-link fencing to the two of them. Buster's stumpy tail wagged away in slow time as he knew he had heard that one before. I always seemed to end up being distracted by something going on in the clinic, and my promised 'Bustie' visits always ended up being delayed.

For many of my visits to Kabul, I found that I had no designated place to sleep and so often I would find myself with a makeshift bed in the room next to the clinic, with Buster curled up on a mostly chewed mat on the floor by the side of my bed, whilst Foxy, the cute little tan-coloured pup, snuggled up on the bed covers against the outline of my legs.

We had found Buster injured and alone on the estate one morning, blood congealing around a wound deep in his right thigh that was causing him to limp severely. His ears had been savagely cropped short. Except for his off-white and grey colourings, he looked the spit of Nowzad – the same age and size made him the original dog's doppelgänger, and my heart strings had been well and truly pulled.

Foxy had arrived as an orphan pup and, by accident, as Buster had been in the clinic being treated at the same time, we had realised instantly that Buster had taken a liking to the scared youngster as he gently prodded and licked its tiny body clean. Since that day, they had never been separated. Buster adored looking after the vulnerable pup as she grew up, and played the role of both parents extremely well.

Exploratory examinations of Buster's injury had revealed a bullet lodged in the muscle of his leg. He had been lucky. Maybe it had been a ricochet rather than a direct entry, we really didn't know. But the op to remove it had been pretty straightforward and, after a few weeks of forced rest – which Buster had no trouble adapting to – he had made a complete recovery. He loved nothing better than delivering his trademark *woof* as strangers approached the clinic and so Louise had decided there and then to make both him and Foxy, inseparable as they were, the resident clinic dogs, doing their bit to protect the house and clinic while everybody slept.

I bounded up the two short steps, across the threshold and into the cramped clinic.

Dr Hadi was standing by the surgical table, his back to me, hands spread flat on the smooth metal table as if in deep thought. He didn't turn to greet me as he normally did each morning, and nor was there any of the normal exchange of pleasantries about our respective families. And that for an Afghan meant only one thing: something was wrong.

I grabbed a much-needed bottle of water from the fridge and, as I opened it, quickly scanned the room as I walked around the table to face Dr Hadi.

My heart sank as I saw the source of his – and now my – problem.

My passion had always been to make a difference for the dogs of Afghanistan and, to be honest, I had not initially given much thought to the Afghan cat population until I had met Louise. Her first-ever rescue had obviously involved a cat and so providing some sort of facilities for the welfare of cats out in Afghanistan was now very much part of our operation.

Louise had been extremely chuffed by the bank of wooden cat cages that, along with the forced labour provided in the form of Dr Norm, had been constructed some weeks earlier. Testing their DIY skills to the limit, their labour of love had saved us a fair sum of money in the process. Standing two cages high and four cages across, each individual cage contained a mid-level shelf so that the cat had the opportunity to spend their time over two levels if they so wished. The entire front of each cage was a door of chicken-wire within a frame, hinged on one side and secured on the opposite side with a top and bottom brass bolt.

Being made of wood, however, was less than ideal. The danger was of cross-contamination from the previous occupant to the next, as bacteria could easily soak into the porous wood. Which left Juma, our very shy but extremely hardworking 'cat guy' as we affectionately called him, with an epic cleaning job on his hands every day. But he never complained. He just made them spotless. Professional, clinical, stainless-steel cat-holding cages were on our wish list, but we knew we would have to win the fundraising lottery for that to become a reality any time soon. So, for now, it had to be the wooden-built cat cages.

However, due to the enthusiastically homemade nature of the cages, a few doors were just slightly out of kilter with their frames. Which meant that with the two left-hand cages, closing them properly was slightly tricky, as the door would jam before it was closed properly, leaving the locking bolts at times impossible to ram home. With all the cages in constant use, forcing the bolts home had begun to take its toll on the screws holding the bolts in position.

I had thought about replacing the bolts on the two cages only the day before. I had noticed they were probably about to fall off – one bolt was even missing two of the four screws that it required. I just hadn't got around to it.

I hadn't even had a gulp of the opened bottle of water in my hand. I took a deep breath – the day had just got worse. Much worse.

Wylie's antics were instantly forgotten as I asked, 'Where is the cat?' as calmly as possible. I was staring into a cage now devoid of its feline occupant, the dish of barely touched cat food and the crumpled blanket now without purpose, the wonky wooden door wide open.

With zero response from Dr Hadi forthcoming, I repeated the question. Still no response.

I exhaled slowly. 'Count to ten,' I thought to myself.

I scanned the clinic once more, the jumbled boxes of animal medicines, bandages and medical instruments overflowing from our limited storage space. There was no sign of the tabby cat that had just arrived with us for two weeks of boarding while her owner travelled home for a well-deserved break back to the United Kingdom.

Dr Hadi avoided eye contact as he cleared his throat but failed to speak.

Just for my complete peace of mind I asked again, this time in my limited Farsi: *'Kojâ hast peshak?'*

I waited patiently for him to reply.

Dr Hadi's grasp of the English language was very good – a few minor grammatical errors now and again, but he most definitely had understood my question. In both of the languages I had used.

His continued silence answered my question. My heart began to sink.

I could see by the confused lines etched across the face of our head vet that he had no idea. Instead, the open wooden door of a completely empty cat cage painted the picture a thousand words from Dr Hadi could not have told me.

I turned and looked at the open door to the outside world I had only moments before walked through. 'Oh, shit.' I put the still undrunk bottle of water down on the table and joined Dr Hadi in staring into space.

The world, I knew, was very unforgiving and would be most likely fatal for a socialised cat that had not been through the Afghan street cat survival course required of all ferals to make it to adulthood in this country.

The owner had originally rescued it as a kitten. The cat had grown up knowing nothing but love and affection, living as a full-time house cat in the accommodation where the owner lived whilst employed in her role at the United Nations.

'The cat has escaped, hasn't it?' I said, stating what I knew was the bleeding obvious. I rolled my eyes upwards. 'We're in trouble.'

On my watch, we had just lost a cat. And not just a stray, but a well-looked-after house cat who belonged to somebody who, without question, adored the cat. I remembered clearly stating several times to the owner as she dropped off the cat: 'Don't worry, we will take great care of Tibbles. Please go and enjoy your two weeks back home.'

I had said it several times, in fact.

With a smile.

'Oh, *shit*.' For the second time. I really didn't rate the chances of survival for the cat. There were too many natural predators out there, and when you included 'man' in the equation, the odds were stacked firmly against a friendly cat being able to survive.

My mind raced with possibilities.

The cat had had at least an hour's head start.

'Right,' I ordered in my best former Royal Marine sergeant's voice, 'Dr Hadi, please get all of the staff here *now*.'

He looked at me questioningly.

'Now, please, Dr Hadi.' My voice was raised but not yet at anger volume.

Losing a cat that we had been entrusted to look after would be very damaging for our emerging reputation as a professional animal welfare charity in Afghanistan. Not to add that Louise would *kill* me.

Painfully. And very slowly.

Within minutes of the last of several frantic-sounding phone calls, Dr Hadi had assembled our full complement of Afghan staff in work that day. Wassah, Safi, Khan and Juma all huddled around the wonky operating table, all smiling insanely as I briefed them on my flimsy plan to find the cat.

Blackadder had been one of my favourite TV series when a young Marine. I had always wanted to devise a plan where I could mimic Blackadder's famous line: 'A plan so cunning you could put a tail on it and call it a weasel.' However, this was not going to be that moment. The moment was too serious. And I was not sure we could even really call it a plan, it was so sketchy. But it was the best option I could come up with at that time.

'Split up and search the whole of the estate,' I explained slowly so that Dr Hadi could listen and translate my words into Dari.

That was my plan.

From the pained look on the assembled staff's faces, it seemed they agreed it wasn't that solid either.

They knew, just as I did, that the cat could be anywhere. But, as one, they turned to file out of the door – a lack of urgency apparent.

'If you have to, offer a reward of $10 to any of the locals who find the cat,' I added for good measure, as if I hadn't actually finished the briefing already and their judgmental stares had been too premature. 'Go, go on!' I chided them, clapping my hands for effect and stamping my feet.

Ten dollars to the majority of people born in Afghanistan was a serious amount of money. And it suddenly dawned on me that there was now a serious risk of every stray tabby within a five-mile radius being collected up and dumped at my door, grubby hands outstretched, eagerly awaiting their ten-dollar finder's fee.

And I'd bet another ten dollars that the cat I needed them to find would not be among those caught.

The search party duly left with orders not to return until the cat was safely back in the cage, with new screws firmly in place. I knew it was a tall order. The cat could most definitely be anywhere, and I didn't hold out much hope for locating it.

I briefly surveyed the opened cage one more time and then joined the search, the opened but undrunk bottle of water forgotten and still standing on the operating table.

We searched *everywhere*. Three hours ticked slowly by as desperation began to take over. I personally had probably covered at least four miles by wandering in and out of rundown buildings, searching in every conceivable hiding spot.

The old, disused toilet block had been my least favourite spot to check and one that my staff had avoided without hesitation. I couldn't blame them: the awful smell was overpowering. But I could not avoid checking inside. The rows of evenly spaced cubicles, with a standing pad around the usual hole in the floor that tested your aiming ability pretty well, especially if you wore sandals, led to a universal collection pit out the back. From the state of the place I was probably correct in assuming that on the day of its decommissioning, it had not been cleaned out for a final time. And, worse still, by the looks of it for some it was still very much in use.

I returned to the clinic desperate for that forgotten bottle of water – we had chosen a 41°C day to run around like idiots chasing a cat, and the midday sun was now brutal.

As I arrived back at the clinic, Dr Hadi was already there, offering me a tepidly warm bottle of water as I greeted him. The depressingly still-open and very empty cat cage answered any questions I was about to ask.

I glanced over at Dr Hadi. 'Can you get me the cat's file, please?'

I needed the owner's contact details. It was time to let them know we had lost the cat.

I reluctantly made the call to the owner. It was brief, and I didn't actually do much of the talking. I apologised a fair bit. It was not something I ever wanted to have to do again.

I could hear the tears at the other end of the line. The owner had trusted us with her animal and we had betrayed that trust.

We had spent long hours trying to instil a sense of responsibility for the clients' animals in our staff. It was important they realised the weight they carried on their shoulders, caring for animals that belonged to other people.

I leant against the battered operating table with my head in my hands, anger at losing the cat bubbling away beneath the surface.

Wassah walked in through the open clinic door, his blue T-shirt stained with sweat. Without the need for anybody to say anything, he immediately realised the cat was still missing. He promptly joined myself and Dr Hadi in silent reflection.

He too knew very well that we had screwed up.

After all the love and attention the owner had given in order to take care of the cat, which would have included an exhausting routine of bottle-feeding every few hours during its initial first few weeks – we had just let it walk out of the door.

The silence was deafening.

My head was pounding.

The silence continued.

Scratch, *scratch*, *scratch*.

'What was that?' I asked as we all looked up, startled.

As one, our eyes homed in on the source of the noise: a cardboard box on the highest shelf of the clinic, balanced neatly on top of unused bandages.

With the lightning speed of Bruce Lee, I stuck out my left foot and kicked the clinic door firmly shut with a heavy thud. At the same time Dr Hadi, being the tallest of us present, reached up to gently lift the box from the shelf.

I didn't know about the others, but I dared not hope in case I jinxed what happened next.

Dr Hadi flipped back the cardboard flap and revealed an unfazed tabby cat, curled up tightly, staring up at us and clearly oblivious to the events of the previous three hours, having probably slept through them.

The relief was overwhelming.

'The cat didn't even leave the clinic?' I couldn't believe it.

Jubilantly shaking Wassah's hand as all three of us laughed, the thought occurred to me that we should have actually searched the clinic first before I had ordered everybody out to search the estate. And I couldn't believe we had also left the clinic door wide open during the search. How had the cat not escaped?

We had been lucky. Very lucky. This time I would be happy to call the owner, even if I was somewhat embarrassed.

I had just picked up the phone to make the call as the first, smiling Afghan boy arrived, determined to collect his ten-dollar reward, an unhappy-looking tabby cat contained securely in a wooden crate under his arm.

chapter 18

Airport Run

It was hot. Really hot. The air was absolutely still, the usual dry *shomali* winds from the northern plains painfully absent from the dust-choked and congested streets and alleyways of Kabul.

As the tyres of the Corollas driving ahead of us crunched over the bone-dry dirt roads, churning up dust clouds that obscured our view ahead, I wondered how Wahidullah was able to see well enough to drive. Added to this discomfort was the fact that the air conditioning in our battered SsangYong Istana van had long ceased working. I chuckled mirthlessly to myself as I cranked the window handle to fill the van's interior with cooling, fresh air but instead instantly filled the van with billowing dust particles. The make of the van, in Malay, actually means 'palace'. We were apparently travelling in a moving palace. With the rear seats removed for storage, the bare leather seats we were sitting on ripped and torn, and the suspension shot long ago, the name didn't really feel very apt. Our 'palace' had most definitely seen many a better day.

I looked across at Wahidullah as dust swirled around us both, and shrugged. He just grimaced back with the same resigned look.

We had no choice. It was either that or bake. Every time we pulled to a stop at the many junctions and roundabouts en route, the van became a sauna on wheels, even with the windows open. I tightened the blue-and-white checked head scarf I wore, wrapping it around my head and covering my mouth in imitation of Wahidullah in his vain attempt to breathe.

Kabul being split into many districts, each generally run by one man, means that the layers of autocracy to negotiate can be daunting if you actually want to implement any development or improvements. Especially as most of those in the chain of command generally want to take plaudits for a job well done without actually putting any effort in initially. And even then it could be all dependent on whether, ultimately, the senior official responsible has curried favour with the minister in charge of whichever department responsible for the improvements or developments being pursued. It could be, and generally always was, a complicated mess. Which meant that for our journey today, some roads were paved and some were not. Thankfully, the majority of our route to the airport was on tarmac roads, and I took some comfort from knowing the dust storm would not last too long.

'Sorry, guys, about the dust.' I craned my neck to look behind into the cargo hold of the van. The dust was swirling around in the open space of the rear of the van too, leaving a fine covering on everything. The two dog-transport crates, one distinctly larger than the other, occasionally clattered together as Wahidullah misjudged avoiding a pothole.

Wylie and AJ made no sound in reply.

I would have loved to have been able to let them both ride up on the front seat, free to watch through the side windows the hustle of Kabul as we sped past on route for the airport and their one way ticket to quarantine in the United Kingdom. Maybe in England they could have rode up front – but not here in Kabul. Being stopped at a police checkpoint would have been an epic. All too often, the young Afghani policemen would yank open the side door to a vehicle and start searching the contents inside before the passengers up front had even been allowed to hand over identity papers to the checkpoint commander. If a dog had been loose in the back of the vehicle, especially Houdini dog Wylie himself, then we would have been in trouble.

Being stopped several times a day as you drove in and out of the so-called 'police ring of steel' surrounding all the main thoroughfares into Kabul city was par for the course. And, along with the majority of the population, if it kept the Taliban out of the city then I was OK with that.

It just meant that any of our dogs being transported to the airport were crated from start to finish. It was safer for them.

Our road passed a former grain silo on the left, now abandoned and settling into its ruinous fate. The upper walls of the factory had been severely damaged from the impact of several rocket-propelled-grenade attacks, along with hundreds of random bullet holes that pock-marked around a long-since shattered window on the top floor. I guessed it had been the scene of a desperate last stand – from which side I had no idea: the coalition, Taliban or Northern Alliance? I did know, though, that with that amount of firepower directed towards the window, I wouldn't have fancied my odds alone up there.

This stretch of road was thoroughly neglected: I doubted it had been repaired in several years as we bounced and juddered along, narrowly avoiding the cars nearest to us with mere millimetres to spare as everybody attempted to steer clear of the largest of the potholes.

My initial shock and nervousness at realising that there was no lane discipline when driving around Kabul had very quickly been replaced by real fear when experiencing games of Corolla car chicken. Just because we happened to be driving in one direction on the correct side of the road apparently didn't stop any other driver from heading towards us, rapidly and in our lane.

'They are on our side of the road,' I would state calmly, for the record. Just to remind Wahidullah. Or maybe we were actually on his side of the road? Who knew? But no matter, because . . . 'Wahidullah, Wahidullah!' My voice would become more high-pitched as my fingers tightened on the dashboard, the full beard and brown *pakul* head dress of the owner of the swiftly approaching car growing larger by the second.

'Mr Pen, all good.' Wahidullah would actually take his eyes off the road to turn and look at me whilst he said it.

Miraculously though, we never crashed. And, even more unbelievably, we had yet to even collect any souvenir scratches from the majority of less than careful road users around us.

Tackling a roundabout in the city, however, was a whole new level of fear to be experienced. And there were many roundabouts in Kabul. I had long decided to either play with my phone or watch daily life in the city pass me by through the passenger side window, and ignore Kabul's unique Highway Code. Always with the hope rather than the belief that we would come out the other side unscathed.

Wahidullah just took it all in his stride and, just like all the other drivers on the road, cursed and blasted the horn to show his non-appreciation of what he clearly assessed to be driving skills far inferior to his own.

There was an audible *clunk* now, and then the welcome, continuous sound of our tyres running over smooth tarmac as we left the dust-cloud-plagued tracks behind.

Alongside the road were clustered groups of street vendors, a bounty of colourful parasols sheltering the goods and sellers from the debilitating rays of the intense afternoon sun. The streets were now predominantly filled with men going about the daily chores. It was rare to even see women shopping. Afghan culture was taking time to return to the norms of the pre-Soviet era.

Once again, I marvelled at the variety and range of items you could buy in Kabul. Everything was for sale and everything had a negotiable price. The wooden wheeled stalls, now set up in stationary mode, were adorned with their commodities for sale. We pulled up opposite a young boy in his dust-streaked *salwar kameez*, dusting off the row upon row of neatly stacked cans of Red Bull and Monster energy drinks amongst the smaller cans of orangeade, lemonade and Coca-Cola, all invitingly waiting to quench the thirst of the many customers who would be visiting that day.

Wahidullah leaned past me and indicated for the young boy to approach. I smiled at the dark-haired lad as he came up to the vehicle and gave him the best-pronounced '*Salam*' that I could.

The kid just stared at me with his dark eyes, his expression unchanged.

I looked towards Wahidullah: 'Your turn,' I said, as I leant back so that he could speak directly to him.

Wahidullah's everyday Dari was too fast for me to follow. I caught the words for 'water' and 'bottles', but nothing else.

The young entrepreneur didn't grab a bottle from the wooden stall's display but bent down low to reach under the shade of the stall itself, producing a worn blue cool box. Inside were several bottles of water nestling between clumps of melting ice. An incredibly welcome sight.

Handing tattered Afghani notes over in exchange for the bottles, we pulled away from the kerb as I began hastily peeling the plastic seal from the bottles' tops.

I wished Wylie and AJ could see what was going on as we passed sellers parading boards containing hundreds of designer sunglasses, their highly polished lenses dazzlingly enticing young Afghan men and teenage boys to try a pair on. You could clearly see the influence from Afghan's love affair with Bollywood on display as we drove around Kabul. Many stalls were laden with stack after stack of Bollywood DVDs. The DVD jacket would feature pictures of colourful, scantily clad Indian women draped around buff, macho-looking Indian male leads.

Nearly all young Afghan men and teenage boys in the city dressed as the male lead from one of the over-the-top Indian action films: highly polished black shoes, tight blue jeans and a flamboyant, open-neck shirt, their gleaming black hair immaculately gelled into position. The footballer Ronaldo was a hairdressing icon in Kabul, his image displayed in nearly all the barber shop windows we passed. I wondered if he knew of the following he had amongst the youth of Afghanistan. Even the growing of beards, a former iconic symbol of the Taliban regime, was in rapid decline as early as just a few years after the fall of the Taliban. The youth of Kabul was very much clean shaven: I actually stood out when I did grow a beard.

These male grooming traits, however, were not to impress Afghan women. With a culture that chose for you who you were to marry and a society with no social forums for unrelated men and women to acceptably be allowed to mingle together, there was not much point in wasting time attempting to impress a member of the opposite sex. Even at weddings women were kept to one room and the men another. So the men dressed to impress their male peers. Afghan traditional dress was reserved for Afghani special occasions or was the preserve of the old men who knew no different.

We turned onto the airport road, the traffic intensifying as we reached the heavily armed first checkpoint we needed to pass through in order to enter Kabul International Airport.

Travelling through any airport these days requires a certain 'Just accept it' attitude. Doing what you are asked at every security checkpoint, sometimes to the point of frustration, is just part of the safety chain.

It is still too mind-boggling to think about the impact of 9/11. Whilst so many people lost their lives that day, I try to offset the thoughts of sadness and despair with the minuscule positives that have since come about. It will never compensate for the terrible atrocity that happened, but it can be some small, very small, compensation, I find.

9/11 changed a lot of things – my life among them and, I'm sure, for many of you reading this book. If the airport security checks at Boston's Logan International Airport had picked up the terrorists before they had boarded the flight, there would be no Nowzad Dogs charity, as I would never have been deployed to Afghanistan. There would have been no Royal Marine sergeant to rescue Nowzad and Tali, and Wylie would have continued to wander Kandahar alone, if he had survived his final attack at all. Louise would have stayed working in Iraq until the security work dried up and then gone on to do who knew what. And, thinking about it, I would never have met Hannah on the slopes of a mountain in Morocco, and who would then crazily give up a successful career in the road-building industry to accompany me to Afghanistan and take on the challenge of promoting animal welfare in a country fighting to come into the modern world.

Travelling to New York with Hannah, who had by then become my girlfriend, to give a talk to promote American fundraising support for the work of the charity, we found ourselves with a day free in New York City. I knew what I wanted to do. And Hannah was pleased to accompany me.

The 9/11 Memorial occupies eight acres of the site of the former World Trade Center's twin towers. Where the footprints of the two towers once stood now lie two 30ft-deep, one-acre pools in honour of the innocent who went to work that day and never came home.

Set amongst young saplings, it is a place for reflection and thought.

We took in the museum and marvelled at the heroics and bravery of the NYC firemen who were still running up the stairs as the buildings collapsed. The glass case containing the shattered helmet of Firefighter Christian Waugh was a sobering reminder of the destructive forces involved, ones that nobody could ever have imagined. Our lads in Helmand never ran into a burning building but, for some, their protective equipment never saved them either. I touched the case's glass. It was cold to touch and a shiver went down my spine.

Thoughts of a time and place, now just a memory, came flooding back.

Helmand never leaves you.

Entering 'Ground Zero' through the security checkpoints every visitor is required to go through, was another reminder of the constant paranoia that America now experiences daily. The sad fact is that Al Qaeda achieved its aim, and fear has replaced the old complacency.

We walked solemnly through the open, concreted areas towards the first of the two enormous pools. Other tourists walked quietly around us but none, I figured, was here to do what I was going to do.

The names of all those who perished inside the towers are etched into the surrounding marble tops of the sunken pools. The spray from the waterfalls dropping 30ft to the surface below was blowing up and finely covering those silently reading the names. Nobody seemed to register it. The dead deserve complete focus.

Hand in hand, we walked to the furthest north-east corner of the memorial park and stood by the marble topped sunken pool representing the northern tower. It was quiet and peaceful. With no security in view, I took off my rucksack and undid the zipper to reach the contents inside.

I had smuggled in a small bottle of red wine and two plastic cups. I quickly poured the wine.

I stood to face the memorial. Two of my Marines had not come home from Afghanistan. 'Marine Richie Watson and Marine Ben Reddy,' I stated simply. We both touched cups in salute and drank slowly, savouring the taste of the wine while I reflected on the scale of what had happened, and the ripples that were still being felt years after.

The world had changed drastically because of what had happened at this very spot. To actually understand fully the implications of that September day was overwhelming.

And now, as I got out of the van for the third time in less

than 400 yards, adopting the spread-eagle legs and raised arms position in anticipation of being searched again, I just smiled to myself as I said, '*Salam*,' to the sweating police officer who was about to pat me down. Targeting the airport would have been a massive coup for the Taliban leadership, with their PR office in Quetta and Twitter accounts to publicise the battle with the foreign occupiers and 'puppet government' of Kabul. Being searched was just something that happened these days, and being anything other than compliant was just stupid.

As we turned away from entering the passenger car park at the airport terminal and headed towards the cargo buildings we were stopped, yet again, by the guard to the cargo road, the steel arm of the red-and-white striped barrier rigidly blocking our progress.

Exchanging greetings, the guard then proceeded to – just as every other guard had done before – yank open the van's sliding rear passenger door to see what we were transporting.

Wylie reacted as I had expected, and violent barking answered the policeman's curiosity.

Even though it was plain to see what we were transporting, the guard still choose to rattle the crate that he was travelling in.

'*Do sag!*' I shouted to be heard above the barking that there were just two dogs.

The policeman withdrew from the rear of the van and came to stand next to the open driver's window. A short, sharp conversation between Wahidullah and the guard followed.

We had to date, as a charity, reunited over 500 companion cats and dogs with the soldiers who had first taken care of the animals on the front lines of Afghanistan. Which meant we had to endure this airport trip all too often.

Wahidullah looked at me now, embarrassment clearly evident on his face. 'He wants fifty Afghani,' he stated simply.

Bribes are a big part of Afghan society, and corruption is sadly all too commonplace. Both myself and Louise had agreed vehemently that we would not contribute to the bribe culture if we could help it as we strove to make progress with animal welfare in Afghanistan, but an airport run was different. We were on a clock.

If we didn't pay then the guard would hold us at the barrier until a superior arrived. I wasn't at all concerned about being sent to an Afghan jail – we had the correct paperwork to pass – but holding us until it was all sorted out would be the guard's warped perception of paying us back for not paying him. By the time it had all been squared away, we would have missed the cargo clearance inspection, Wylie and AJ would not fly and the charity would be out of pocket. And I was all too well aware of the bollocking I would receive from Louise if I brought both dogs back to the shelter, after all the effort it had taken to book their flights.

'OK, my friend,' I said reluctantly to Wahidullah. 'Pay him *penjâ* Afs.'

The policeman was topping up his meagre pay, so I guess I couldn't blame him too much. He no doubt assumed that if westerners had money to waste on flying dogs out of Afghanistan, then they could spare what amounted to about a dollar for him to lift the barrier.

The cargo hall itself was a huge, cavernous shell of a building. Most of the floor that day was taken up with bundles of tightly wrapped carpets, a percentage of which was currently being untied by Afghan workers, who were spreading them out across a not exactly clean tarp laid out on the floor in anticipation of the forthcoming customs inspection.

The cargo hall manager was waiting to greet us. I liked him. He was always polite and always wore a suit. Walking with a slight limp, he spoke perfect English and seemed to enjoy the thorough questioning I subjected him to as I strove to discover more about Afghan society once we had been through the formal customs inspection, as we waited for the flight line cargo truck to arrive.

The formal inspection proceeded as it normally did, with a smartly dressed customs official ordering me to remove Wylie from his travel crate.

I bent down to press carefully the travel-crate door-release clips with my right hand, a dog lead fashioned into a noose in the other.

'OK, Wylie. Play the game, buddy,' I said as soothingly as I could, as I carefully opened the crate door.

As soon as Wylie heard the metal bolts pull back he attempted to scramble out to freedom, but I had thought ahead and my left knee was already in place to block him as I swiftly dropped the noose lead over his head.

'Gotcha, Houdini boy!' I exclaimed as I let him trot off to smell the corner of the cargo hall, my left hand grasping the lead as tightly as I could, whilst the official, who had now donned a pair of latex gloves, proceeded to inspect the interior of the travelling crate.

Even with the war on terror and thousands of American and coalition troops on the ground in Afghanistan, year on year the opium trade is growing across Afghanistan as demand around the world for those who want to shove white powder up their noses so they could have a perceived good time increases. To satisfy demand, the Afghan warlords who control the poppy cultivation have to transport their products out of the country somehow, and no one is exempt from suspicion.

Once he was satisfied the crate was clean, the official signalled for me to come back with Wylie. It was time for the dog pat-down.

I was always wary of this part of the procedure as I never knew how the dog would react to an Afghan customs officials – who generally did not like dogs and were never overly happy with the thought of actually having to touch one.

Dogs always sensed this and normally played up to it.

'No funny business, Wylie,' I chided him as I crouched down to cup his head in the crook of my left arm and held him tightly to my body with my right. It was a bear hug of sorts and one I could control him in if Wylie decided to freak out.

The official waited for another few seconds to reassure himself that I had Wylie under control and then he nervously leant forwards and quickly examined around Wylie's stomach and head, prodding here and there in case we had somehow stuffed bags of heroin into a live dog.

We hadn't.

I guided Wylie back into his Sky Kennel and started the procedure all over again with AJ. I smiled inwardly at the discomfort that appeared on the customs official's face as AJ's big head thrust out of the entrance to the travel crate.

'Slowly, AJ. Wait a minute,' I said as I struggled to hold him still long enough to put the lead around his thick neck.

Wahidullah was already carefully threading cable ties in and out to secure Wylie's travel crate door to avoid any mid-air Houdini-style stunts.

I missed with the lead the first time and AJ took it as a signal to launch out of the kennel.

'Whoa, AJ! Steady,' I stressed as I grabbed him around the neck and reeled him back towards me, almost losing my balance in the process.

The customs official had seen enough, however, and wasn't risking getting close enough to what he perceived as an out-of-control dog.

'Finish,' he ordered, as he gestured for AJ to go back into the Sky Kennel. Without waiting to see if I had understood, he turned on his heel and stormed away, pulling the latex gloves from his fingers with distaste.

AJ was close enough to my head as we watched the chap walk away that I felt a slobbery tongue lick clear up my right cheek.

'Nice one, mate,' I said smiling, as I ruffled his big, daft head.

Wahidullah just looked on, perplexed at the interaction us westerners had with the dogs under our care.

I gently pushed AJ back into the crate and thankfully he backed up. During previous customs visits, not all of our rescued dogs had been overly happy at being forced back into a restrictive travel crate. I always won, but had the scars to prove it.

'Good lad, Wylie. It'll be over soon.' I tried my best to reassure him, as I could see anxiety in the way he was standing in the small crate. He had been as good as gold.

Wahidullah checked the cable ties whilst I slipped him a biscuit through the metalled mesh cage door of his Sky Kennel. Thankfully, Wylie had seemed fairly unfazed by the inspection and tucked into his biscuit.

'Enjoy it – no more for a few hours yet,' I thought to myself. Both dogs faced at least five hours in their crates until they would be let out into the animal transit facility at Dubai airport.

We waited in the relative coolness of the cargo hanger for the airline truck to arrive. The carpets had long since been inspected and carefully rerolled into neat bundles once more.

I had topped up Wylie's water container, which was secured to the inside of his door, by pouring water through the bars of the crate door. Wylie had lapped at the water immediately, probably after the dryness of the biscuit.

Eventually, a rusting flatbed truck arrived to collect our precious cargo for the late afternoon flight to Dubai. After a cursory look at the many copies of the health certificates and airway bills we were obliged to provide for the dogs' flights, they were gently loaded on to the back of the truck.

I always felt sad saying goodbye to the dogs we helped rescue for the soldiers I never met. Wylie poked his wet nose through the gaps in the crate door, his eyes looking longingly out towards me. He was eye-level with me now that his crate was up on the bed of the truck. But there would no escaping for Wylie this time. Wahidullah had gone overboard securing the door with plastic cable ties.

I again pushed my index finger into the crate and attempted a mini-stroking action to reassure him, against the side of his head. AJ seemed fine – if he was already asleep.

'It's OK, Wylie,' I whispered as the truck started up. 'You're going to a better place, and I'll see you there, all right?' As if he could understand me. I knew it was quarantine but anything was better than here for a dog. He replied with a series of short, sharp barks as the truck pulled away.

'I really hate this part,' I thought to myself. Louise always hated saying goodbye to the dogs, too. We knew that, in most cases, after having looked after them for probably the best part of three months, we would never see them again.

Wahidullah and I watched the truck depart for the airfield, Wylie's barks fading to nothing as the truck turned the corner to the secure cargo entrance to the flight line.

I sighed. 'Come on.' I nodded to Wahidullah. 'Chai time.' We knew a little Afghan chai house on the way back to the shelter.

Wahidullah smiled and nodded happily. While Louise expected us to come straight back so that she could hand over the next job on the list, I figured what she didn't know wouldn't hurt her.

As we strolled away from the cargo hall, I took one last look towards the flight line for signs of Wylie, but the truck had long since disappeared between the rows of parked aircraft.

Wylie, along with AJ, was leaving Afghanistan.

They would never be coming back.

chapter 19

Milo

Standing in the ring on the perfectly green artificial grass, Sarah was nervous. A fairly decent crowd of spectators, sitting on green plastic, foldaway chairs surrounding the ring, was held back by a quarter-height, white-picket fence, the sort you would see on a typical front lawn in the suburbs of America.

Everyone was watching intently.

Dressed in knee-length black boots with jeans, a floral-patterned blouse and long green cardigan, a finalist's rosette pinned to her chest, Sarah quickly eyed up the competition without making it too obvious that that what she was doing.

Deciding on an outfit to wear had been tough. She had flicked through her wardrobe at home before travelling up to London for the event, pondering the pros and cons of each outfit and how it would come across in the arena. Nothing too casual but, then again, she didn't want to come across as overdressed.

Trying to put herself in the shoes of the judges, she guessed her main rival was the woman in the black leggings and denim shorts wearing a pair of brown Ugg boots. She was standing to the right, her hair pulled back tightly into a ponytail that dropped down the left side of her head.

Sarah looked down the line of the other finalists. Most were slouching. Sarah was a stickler for standing upright and proud and, with her own cardigan ensemble being more appropriate than the denim shorts to her right, she reckoned she had this.

Sarah quickly focused back towards the judges, flashing her best cheesy smile at them and a more confident one to her loyal fan base, who had accompanied her to the event and who were hollering away like crazy.

The announcer, a jolly chap proudly sporting his red poppy for Remembrance was currently leading the entourage of esteemed judges along the line of finalists, introducing each hopeful woman to the audience.

It was going to be a tough group of judges to impress. There was the actor, Anthony Head, most famous for his role as the librarian guardian in *Buffy the Vampire Slayer*. Dressed in a black suit, he was carefully eyeing each finalist in turn, then standing back quietly while he pondered their story. With him, and enthusiastically clapping and encouraging the audience to join in every time the announcer called out a finalist's name, was the dynamic duo of JoAnne Good and Anna Webb, hosts of the fast-paced London radio show *Barking at the Moon*. Between the three of them they were under pressure to come to a unanimous decision as to the outright winner, right there in front of the gathered audience.

Sarah's pulse quickened as the announcer swept up to her, mike held close to his mouth as he introduced her over the tannoy system to the fascinated spectators. She imagined all eyes were on her as, taking a deep breath, she smiled at the team of judges as they surrounded her. Sarah was the last of the finalists in line so, after a few pleasantries had been exchanged, they moved off back to the centre of the ring to huddle closely in conference.

Briefly, time stood still.

Anthony Head looked across once more at the line-up before turning back to an animated JoAnne who was clearly pushing her champion. Anna nodded politely as she listened to Anthony voice the merits of his chosen candidate.

The announcer looked at his watch. Obviously fully aware of the strict timetable he was required to adhere to, he thrust the mike into the midst of the debating judges.

'So, Anthony?' he asked, pushing along the decision-making process. 'What are your thoughts on our finalists?' His voice echoed from the speakers secured to the large hall's ceiling.

Anthony Head led off first, explaining his thoughts and giving credit to all the finalists anxiously standing waiting in the ring, before both JoAnne and Anna took their turns in saying a few words in front of the hushed crowd.

Then, as one, the three of them turned to face each other and nodded.

'You've reached a decision then?' the announcer asked, as soon as he noticed the judges waiting patiently.

'Yup,' Anthony replied. 'Unanimous decision.'

'Great! So why did you choose the finalist you did?' the announcer asked, prolonging the suspense for the crowd and the now extremely nervous finalists.

Anthony paused for a moment to collect his thoughts and then simply said, 'Well, when the finalist we have chosen entered the ring, we were simply stunned.'

Both Anna and JoAnne nodded in agreement, JoAnne adding: 'It's been an emotional journey to reach this decision.'

Sarah took one last look up and down the line at the other finalists. She didn't want to count her chickens just yet, but she was *sure* she had this. Sarah took in another deep breath and held it.

All three judges counted down together from three to one before then announcing the winner to the waiting world.

It had taken a lot of appearances and being the subject of many a judge's scrutiny for Sarah to make it this far as a finalist at the top show of its kind in London. She was addicted to it, the buzz of the win, having been attending shows since she was a kid growing up in the orchard county of Somerset.

But this was the biggest by far.

The arena fell silent. Sarah knew she had won.

'Milo!' the judges shouted together. 'The winner is Milo!'

The roar of the crowd was deafening.

Sarah let the news sink in for a few seconds before her face broke into an enormous grin. She bent down to congratulate the real star of the ring and the chosen winner: Milo, her big, beautiful English bull terrier cross.

'Well done, Milo!' she called down to him.

With his big bull terrier head, his left eye completely blacked out in a patch of dark hair, making him look like an eye patch-wearing dog pirate, his thin, pointy tail wagged away crazily as Sarah led the big, proud dog forward on his lead towards the judges. Not that the young Milo knew a lot about it, but he had just been crowned, 'The James Wellbeloved Crossbreed Dog of the Year 2011'.

As was the protocol at these types of events, Sarah and Milo were obliged to trot around the outer edges of the ring, Milo's leash in her right hand as Sarah proudly held on to his winner's rosette in the other as the spectators rose to their feet to applaud the worthy winner.

An interview with the *Discover Dogs* television camera crew came next. Whilst Sarah knew she could talk – a lot – she wasn't so sure about doing it in front of a camera. But she needn't have worried: once the camera rolled and the interviewer bombarded her with questions about her passion which was, of course, dogs, Sarah relaxed and fell into the routine of the interview.

'What is Milo actually crossed with?' the female interviewer asked for the benefit of the audience back home.

'Actually, it's 50 per cent bull terrier and 50 per cent Northern Inuit,' Sarah explained as Milo, tail still wagging excitedly away walked around in circles, clearly wishing the run around the ring had lasted a bit longer.

'Why did you enter him?' the interviewer asked as the camera focused in on Milo's big, thick-set head.

'Well, I love dog shows,' Sarah said, completely understating the fact that she was addicted to them. 'And when I realised there was a competition for crossbreeds then this boy here, who wins everything back home, was entered.' As she answered, it was clear that she was unsure whether to look at the interviewer or the camera lens.

The interviewer congratulated Sarah once again for her win and, with the interview finished, Sarah was released to savour the victory of her four-legged canine companion. She knelt down properly to make a fuss of her big dope, Milo. He lovingly licked her face in return.

Now all Sarah had to do was figure out how she would

carry the trophy and the prize of several large bags of dog food, from the competition's sponsor, James Wellbeloved, home on the train with her, whilst keeping tabs on a now completely hyper and very strong English bull terrier cross.

Sarah had been twelve when she had first entered a dog show. It had been part of a local horse show and, as she didn't actually own a dog as her family only owned cats, she had improvised and borrowed one.

A friend of her father's had loaned her his dog for the day and had been pleasantly surprised when the young, determined Sarah had returned some time later in the afternoon with the borrowed dog in tow, and a winner's rosette.

The following year, still with no dog of her own, Sarah had once more borrowed a dog so she could enter the same dog show. The seed had been sown. Sarah was officially a dog-show addict.

Some years later, Sarah still desperately wanted a dog of her own. It was her mum who was still rightly advising against the idea, reminding her daughter of the long hours she spent away at work. After their last conversation on the topic, whilst outwardly Sarah had reassured her mum that she wouldn't get a dog just yet, inwardly she had been cringing inside, knowing that she had actually already acquired a dog via the guy she had been seeing at the time. Sam the collie cross.

For several months, Sarah convinced her mum that the dog actually belonged to her boyfriend's mate and they were just caring for it.

Sam was hard work. With no idea of his previous history, they found looking after him uniquely frustrating. The dog just would not come into the house when called. Sarah and her boyfriend would gently coax Sam in through the back door of the house but as soon as they went to walk past the slightly mad dog to close the door, Sam would turn tail and sprint back into the garden. They then had to start the laborious coaxing game all over again.

There was only one solution. Once the nightmare that was Sam was inside the house, her boyfriend would keep Sam distracted while Sarah climbed out of the living room window and snuck round to firmly close the door on the unsuspecting dog.

Never giving up on Sam, Sarah worked hard to finally get the problem dog to trust her. Her hard work paid off, except for a period of leaving Sarah little smelly presents in the house, and they settled into a proper dog and owner routine.

Time moved on, and Sarah found herself single and the sole owner of Sam. Renting a quaint, gorgeous cottage situated on a sprawling farm complex on the outskirts of Yeovil, Sarah was able to give a loving home to another rescued dog, this time an adorable oldie simply called Ted, a Jack Russell.

Scared of his own shadow, Ted would even hide at the sound of Sarah's friend walking around the house in her new squeaky running shoes. But the wet blanket of a dog was most definitely a cutie and, Sarah discovered to her delight, had a knack for winning dog shows.

Adding to her dog show mileage by travelling to all the events she could, Sarah become a regular. Sam was, although Sarah thought he was gorgeous, in her own words: 'crap at winning events'. And so, taking a friend along with her to look after Sam, the two of them would stand and patiently wait for the inevitable: Ted and Sarah winning.

Ted, although getting on in years, was assumed by everybody to be a young puppy as he was just so energetic, and with a tail that never stopped wagging, ensured he won 'Best Waggy Tail' category or 'Happiest Veteran' at dog shows all over the West Country. He was a born winner.

Losing Ted to a stroke, Sarah was devastated. Her large cottage seemed lonely without the reassuring company of two dogs always by her feet. Sam too, felt the void left by little Ted's departure, and Sarah took the decision to find a companion for Sam to keep him company while she was at work. And, of course, to take on the successful, big shoes left by Ted in the country dog shows.

It was around then that she received a call from a friend who bred English bull terriers.

'Hi Sarah, it's Bindy, I have had a bit of a breeding accident you might want to take a look at!'

Sarah's mind flicked through the many possibilities that could be described as a 'breeding accident'.

'What are you talking about?' Sarah had asked rather worried as to the nature of the reply.

'My English bull terrier accidentally bred with our Inuit!' Bindy quickly explained as Sarah tried to figure out how it accidentally happened. Bindy was a good friend of Sarah's and knew that Sarah had a soft spot for English bull terriers. 'Do you want one?

Leaving home to see what an accidental breeding mishap looked like, Sarah returned home with Milo, the bull terrier-Inuit cross pup, the breeding mishap now apparent.

The fact that Milo was a crossbreed didn't bother Sarah at all. She was very happy to be taking home an English bull terrier cross, half of him was just like Bodger from her favourite childhood film. The Walt Disney classic about three inseparable friends on an unforgettable journey across the Canadian wilderness: *The Incredible Journey* starred the unlikely travelling companions of Tao the Siamese cat, Luath the Labrador Retriever and, of course, Bodger the hulking bull terrier! Sarah had had a soft spot for the lovable, big character of the movie, and she guessed that she had never really forgotten it.

And so Milo, with his black eye patch and sleek pointy ears, moved into the beautiful setting of the Yeovil farm.

But Milo wasn't the success that Sarah had hoped for at first: Ted's charm and good fortune in the ring proved to be unique. And Sarah had set her sights a little higher than just winning the local dog competitions.

Whilst taking part in a small-scale village event, the judge had been particularly taken with the very striking and proud-looking Milo. 'You should definitely show this one properly at big shows,' the judge had stated, matter-of-factly, in a strong Devonshire accent.

Sarah had been confused. 'But he's a crossbreed, so I can't,' she had replied. It was common knowledge that show dogs were all pure breed specimens that were worth hundreds if not thousands of pounds. Milo had cost £150. And she had no interest in showing purebreds. Going all out to win as many dog shows as she could with her motley crew of formerly unwanted canines was her way of sending a message that any dog, whether a rescue or not so popular crossbreed, could be just as rewarding, if not more so, than buying an overly expensive pup from a breeder.

So it was sweet music to her ears when the judge smiled the knowing smile of experience: 'My dear, Scruffts is a Kennel Club competition for crossbreeds. Milo here is an amazing dog and will most definitely do well.' The judge patted the big lad on the head.

Now this was an opportunity Sarah was not going to miss, and she chided herself on not knowing this before. Looking into the requirements for entering Scruffts, she read out the four categories to a bored Milo, who was lying with his head flat on the cold kitchen tiles of the cottage, decidedly uninterested.

'Prettiest Bitch.' Sarah turned her head away from the computer screen to look at the glum and definitely male face of Milo. 'Yeah, don't think so.' She scrolled down further to read the next category out loud: 'Child's Best Friend,' she said, confusion etched on her face. 'I am too old!' Sarah continued to the next heading: 'Golden Oldie.'

Even Milo raised an eyebrow in her direction. He was only three years old.

'OK, I think we have a winner,' she exclaimed as she came to the last category for crossbreeds: 'Most Handsome'. Milo was indeed handsome and, with his eye patch, a very unique dog.

But the judge at the first of several qualifying events, this one in Plymouth, disagreed with Sarah's view of Milo. Sadly, they were not selected to proceed to the next stage of the competition for 'Most Handsome Crossbreed' and therefore no opportunity to take part in the semi-finals presented itself.

Disappointment filled the cottage when they returned 'sans' rosette.

And, as heart-breaking as it was, Milo was unsuccessful the following year too, at a heat in Gloucestershire.

'Are the judges all blind?' Sarah asked a nonplussed Milo as he rode in the back of the car on the way home, having thoroughly enjoyed all the fuss and attention he had received during the show.

But good things come to those who wait and at their third and final try at the heats during the Bath and West Show the gentle dog, who truly had no idea what was going on, finally won the accolade that Sarah had had him earmarked for. Milo was crowned regional 'Most Handsome Crossbreed' and was awarded his place at the finals during the London Discover Dogs show in the November of 2011.

The rest was history. Sarah had known, deep down, that Milo would win the show. She couldn't explain why, but she just knew. In fact Milo, under her careful guidance, had beaten many other deserving crossbreeds to not only win 'Most Handsome' but then go on to win the Grand Final, too.

For any other person addicted to dog shows and happy at being surrounded by their four-legged friends, winning the ultimate dog show should have been the icing on the cake of a glorious rescue-dog 'showing' career.

But not Sarah. Not the girl who had first confidently taken to the ring aged twelve. Although, as she stood in the ring, savouring the moment as the crowd clapped her success, pleased as Punch for her loyal, waggy-tailed companion who was happily trotting by her side as they completed just one more lap, she had absolutely no inkling that her endeavours with Milo were just the beginning.

chapter 20

Quarantine

Melissa stared at Wylie. Wylie stared back at Melissa.

Both sat contemplating their options.

Melissa was intent on getting to Wylie. Wylie actually wanted her to get to him – the bone-shaped biscuits he had spied in her hand convinced him of that. But with the current lie of the land, that was just not going to happen anytime soon.

Quarantine is a prison of sorts for dogs and cats who have done no wrong except come from a rabies-endemic country. A compulsory sentence of six months is given to all dogs arriving in the United Kingdom from non-EU countries that are not part of the costly pet passport scheme, regardless of whether or not they had been vaccinated properly against rabies – as were all the dogs arriving into the care of our Nowzad Dogs shelter. (At the time of writing this book, the United Kingdom no longer has compulsory quarantine if a dog from any country has passed a blood test. In my personal opinion, this is a very bad decision.)

Rabies had more or less been eliminated in the United Kingdom when, back in 1946, with soldiers returning home from war with dogs adopted on the Continent and elsewhere, the government of the day had been forced to act. Thousands of dogs were removed from the returning soldiers to be destroyed, and strict quarantine rules were immediately enforced.

Since 1946 only twenty-five cases of rabies have been recorded in the UK, which sadly also includes British citizens returning to the United Kingdom, who had been bitten by a stray animal whilst on their holidays.

Anybody I had ever spoken to who had been forced to quarantine their four-legged buddy would complain strenuously about the harshness of the experience and the stress it had caused their beloved pet. It's understandable. To grow up as a much-loved family pet, considered as part of the family and more or less present during every aspect of daily life, but then suddenly to be ripped from a family environment and held in solitary confinement for six months was, without doubt, most definitely beyond harsh. Random weekend visits, if the quarantine facility was actually nearby, were restricted to just a few hours to fit in with the quarantine kennel's opening hours. It could be, and normally was, a heart-breaking experience.

It was an unanswerable question. How the hell did you explain to your loyal, loving dog that you were leaving him yet again, when all he wanted to do was come home with you?

I realised that there was a difference for the dogs and cats arriving from Afghanistan: none of them had ever been anybody's pet before. Sure, the soldiers had looked after them and fed them regularly, but the dogs had no routine as such, with most companion animals able to roam free to come and go as they pleased, just as Wylie had been able to do in Kandahar. These dogs and cats were not treated like one of the family, sitting up on the sofa watching television every night, cuddled by their dedicated owner. For the dogs from Afghanistan, arriving into quarantine was the first time they had ever experienced a routine: food was actually brought to them twice a day without them having to scavenge for it or go hungry; friendly interaction with the kennel staff; and, most importantly, and for all of us it was the knowledge that the dogs were now completely safe and not be subject to any form of abuse ever again.

My Nowzad, when he had arrived into the quarantine system in England from Kabul via Islamabad, skinny and covered in blood-sucking ticks, had finally started to put on weight and began to lose his semi-feral ways and gain trust in others. Before it had only been with me. Rebecca and Vicky at the quarantine kennels in London had done a grand job in giving a dog, which before had only ever allowed me to get close to him, the opportunity to realise that other people could be just as caring. In fact, when 24 December 2007 had come around and Nowzad had been given the all clear by the quarantine vet, I truly believe that the cropped-ear former fighting dog was actually sad to leave. I know Rebecca and Vicky shed a tear or two the day I collected him!

For Wylie and AJ, England was just a stopping-off point. To enter Australia so that they could live with their respective saviours, both dogs had to endure six months of quarantine in an approved country prior to arrival in Oz. The day they were both passed as rabies-free in England, they would then have to be put directly onto a flight to Australia so that they could then undertake one more month of in-country approved quarantine.

I found this completely crazy. Both Wylie and AJ had completed the internationally recognised course of 'best practice' rabies vaccination which we implemented as soon as any dog arrived at our facility in Kabul.

But I didn't make the rules. The harsh fact stood: it was what it was. And there was not a damn thing I or anybody else could do about it.

Both dogs had at least seven months of quarantine to do.

The fundraising campaign to pay for all of this had been long and intense. Wylie's story had captured the hearts of our Nowzad supporters far and wide, and all of us had been excited to find out we even had an Australian newspaper coming to our aid to truly promote their stories on an international stage.

And so, with that level of support, we had decided to abandon the quarantine facility on the outskirts of London that we normally used, through no other reason than we wanted to utilise the local support base Wylie had in the West Country. There being no limit to the number of visitors that the dogs could receive during official quarantine opening hours, we would strive to do our best to keep them entertained and active throughout the six months of confinement. If all went well, then Wylie and AJ would be released for collection to travel to meet their flight to Australia on 30 December 2011.

It meant that by the time Wylie was subsequently released from his further one month Australian quarantine, it would be almost one year to the day that the fluffball of a dog, who seemed able to court trouble at every opportunity, had first come to the attention of Danielle back at the battle-weary checkpoint now thousands of miles away.

For all us, it felt like another lifetime ago.

We had all breathed a sigh of relief the day Wylie arrived into the United Kingdom to begin his quarantine. The long flight from Dubai didn't seem to have bothered him and AJ had arrived asleep, just as he had left Afghanistan.

According to the reports I received whilst I was still in Afghanistan, Wylie had taken it all in his stride, strolling out of the Sky Kennel to greet the customs official at Heathrow, before boarding the quarantine vehicle for the long drive west.

Somewhat relieved, we had assumed the hard bit was over.

We assumed wrong. For Wylie, doing anything easy was not part of his make-up.

The kennel at the quarantine was divided into two halves: the first, small section you entered through a heavy metal door directly into the dog's contained sleeping area, which was a raised sleeping platform off to one side, the only light entering through the observation window in the main door. A small hatchway, only barely wide enough for a dog to squeeze through, led to the second half of the kennel. This was the outdoor exercise area for the occupant. About ten feet long, surrounded by a brick wall to waist height, it was completed by a fully enclosed chain-link fence which included a roof. Even Houdini dog himself Wylie was going nowhere. There was a small gate built into the fence to allow cleaning of the outdoor run, but a large padlock prevented unauthorised access.

Melissa was kneeling in the sleeping area of Wylie's quarantine kennel. Wylie was now on the other side of the dog flap in the outdoor exercise area of his run, looking somewhat perplexed that Melissa was not attempting to join him.

'If you want this treat, Wylie, then you have to come back in here,' Melissa pointed out, waving the dog biscuit temptingly from side to side.

When Jess, the duty kennel staffer at the quarantine facility had opened Wylie's kennel door and Melissa had darted inside the bare, cold-looking room to greet him, Wylie had gone into a frantic five minutes of playful madness as he had darted this way, then that, in his excitement at having a visitor.

Finally calming down, Wylie, crazy hair sprouting every which way from the top of his head, sat still long enough – if you can call ten seconds long enough – for Melissa to make a fuss of him: ruffling the crazy, wayward hair on top of his head and rubbing his belly as he fell onto his back, one white-socked paw sticking up in the air. And then, just as suddenly, he had darted headlong through the narrow doorway to his outside domain, leaving Melissa stranded inside.

He had yet to understand that only he could squeeze outside and that if he craved biscuits, then back inside he had to go.

Melissa felt sadness when she thought of what Wylie had endured to get this far. Being of Egyptian descent herself, she knew that animal welfare was mostly non-existent in a Middle Eastern country, especially one like Afghanistan. His crazily wagging quarter-length tail, bright orange eyes and fluffed-up fur coat indicated only one thing: he just wanted to be loved and in human company. Shutting him behind a locked quarantine door after each day's visit ended was heart-breaking.

Melissa had worked for the Nowzad Dogs charity for over

two years, after being semi-poached from the Mayhew Animal
Home in London, a charity that attempted to cope with the
ever-increasing burden of abandoned animals in west London.
Melissa had made the decision to leave the Mayhew reluctantly. But although she had loved the job and her work
colleagues, her childhood sweetheart, Graham, was in
Plymouth and love dictated that she move to the West Country.

The Mayhew had an international arm of its work and had
been instrumental in the initial emails that had pointed me in
the right direction to first rescue Nowzad back in 2007, and I
had given a talk at the Mayhew to thank the staff for the
major-league support I had received from them in fundraising for Nowzad's flight and subsequent quarantine. Melissa
had been in the audience and had been impressed with the
determination and difference that Nowzad Dogs had made in
the relatively short time it had been operating in Afghanistan.
She had also been blown away by the emotional photos that
had brought to life the story of the original dogs of Now Zad,
who had been instrumental in starting the charity's journey.
The colourful stills of the dogs Nowzad, RPG, Jenna, Tali,
AK and Dushka had struck a chord with her after the many
visits with her father back to Egypt and the suffering she had
witnessed there. She had even thought that maybe working
for the Nowzad Dogs charity one day would be something
she could aim for.

What she hadn't realised the day she made the sad decision
to leave the employment of the Mayhew, was that Nowzad
Dogs had needed an experienced hand to take on the newly
acquired charity office in Plymouth. And the charity had, by
coincidence, via Caroline, the CEO of Mayhew, heard that
Melissa would be a very suitable candidate for the job vacancy
they were about to advertise.

What Melissa also had not realised when she eagerly accepted the job, was that working for Nowzad Dogs meant you became a one-man or, in this case, woman, army of multi-tasking madness.

Just because the job description said one thing Melissa soon realised that it meant that she was expected to adapt quickly, to master the ever-mounting list of other responsibilities she was steadily tasked with.

With little funding for anything much other than the animals in Afghanistan, it was all hands to the pump to tackle the burgeoning administration produced by an internationally recognised charity that, in real terms, was still in its infancy. Suddenly, along with her already full day, Melissa had needed to become an expert on the rules and regulations of Australian quarantine, and the planning of all the moving parts that were needed to take two former dogs from the streets and farms of Afghanistan and move them to the almost impenetrable fortress that was Australia. A feat that we had never attempted before.

No one saw the sucker punch that was winding up slowly and which would ultimately delay AJ's move to the beach in Oz.

And completely floor Wylie's chances of a new life in Australia.

chapter 21

Shattered Dreams

The email had come out of the blue. It was direct and to the point, and it sucked. Big time.

I immediately phoned Melissa, who was working from the charity office in Plymouth. If she had been standing next to me I would have probably grabbed hold of her and cried.

She already knew what I was ringing her about.

'Have you seen that email?' I asked, knowing full well she had. I could tell from the drained tone of her voice when she had answered that she too had read it.

For a few seconds the line was quiet, then: 'What are we going to do, Pen?' Melissa asked in reply, the shock in her voice clearly evident.

'I don't know,' I said honestly. To be fair, I was clueless. None of us had even remotely considered the scenario that was now playing out.

The beginnings of a headache was already starting to make itself known at the front of my head. I stared out of the window at the falling snow, my imminently planned dog walk for my lot now on hold indefinitely while I tried to get my head around the unfolding saga. The quaint prospect of a white Christmas did nothing to brighten my mood.

Even after six months of confinement in quarantine, both AJ and Wylie were now unable to travel to Australia.

I couldn't believe it.

I read the email one more time.

Due to the imminent changes within the European Union (EU) to their requirements for the movement of cats and dogs, import conditions for the cats and dogs imported from the UK to Australia also have been changed and the new conditions will be enforced from 1 January 2012.

I understand from your email that the dogs will be completing the UK quarantine requirements on 28 December 2011. However, the Australian quarantine stations will not accept animals until 4 January 2012, so they cannot be exported to Australia before the enforcement of new conditions.

As these animals will be exported in 2012, they must comply with the full Category 4 requirements, including rabies vaccination and rabies anti-body titre testing (RNATT). These dogs will not be eligible for import for 60 days after the date of blood sample collection for RNATT testing. This date determines the quarantine period your animal must perform, from a minimum of 30 days up to 120 days.

To facilitate this, please read through the information package found at the below link, complete the RNATT Declaration attached and forward to AQIS along with the laboratory report. Original documents are not required.

Please note that an AQIS import permit cannot be granted without this information.

The bastards in Australia had changed their import rules to reflect the relaxing of the rules in the UK, but not even the quarantine staff had known of the forthcoming changes.

As Wylie and AJ would finish their quarantine on 28 December, we had assumed they would be accepted into Australia on 30 December, after the exceptionally long 23-hour flight to the other side of the world. We had not even considered that the quarantine station would be closed over the New Year period. Christmas yes, but not New Year. Added to this, Britain had decided to relax its strict, 60-year-old quarantine regime. We had known that was coming. From 1 January 2012 only a passed blood test was required for animals arriving into the United Kingdom. What we hadn't realised was that Australia would change their rules in reply.

Basically, some faceless official was stating that as Wylie and AJ would not be arriving in Australia until four days after the new rules came into effect then, theoretically, the two dogs could be in contact with dogs not up to Australian entry standards who had arrived into the United Kingdom under the new, more relaxed rules.

I was seething. I wanted to punch somebody. Preferably somebody Australian.

The phone call to the Australian quarantine facility in Sydney did nothing to help my mood. They didn't seem to take too kindly to my tone of voice, apparently. And they most definitely didn't seem to have any sympathy with the situation that the dogs were now in. The fact that they had completed six months of quarantine was utterly lost on the official at the other end of the very long line. And their explanation of the process that would now have to be followed was mind-bogglingly complicated.

Ending the call, my resolve to punch an Australian was only stronger. 'Shit!' I said again, for the umpteenth time.

To transport Wylie and AJ to Australia would now require us to start all over again: they would have to do, say, 150 days here in the UK after having their blood tests resubmitted and then 30 days' official quarantine in Australia or 60 days here in the UK, blood tests and then 120 days quarantine in Australia.

The really worrying detail of any scenario would be that if they failed the blood tests that were now compulsory upon arrival in Australia, they would either be returned, at our expense, to the UK, or worse – and a completely unthinkable option – they would be destroyed.

And it wasn't an idle threat. I already knew that Danielle had once helped a working dog called Harry to be returned to Australia. During the quarantine phase at the facility in Sydney, the dog that had served its country in the unforgiving bad lands of Afghanistan had failed to pass the required blood test for leishmaniasis, a nasty disease spread by the bite of the sand fly which was endemic in Afghanistan.

Danielle was given the choice: the dog would be destroyed or returned.

Danielle had known that bringing Harry back to Afghanistan would be a non-starter. So she had fundraised and worked her socks off to find the dog a home in America. And that was where Harry had been flown: all the way from Australian quarantine to the good old United States, which has very minimal entry requirements.

We were now facing a nightmare scenario. I quickly worked out the costs involved. Somehow we now had to fundraise for a further six months of keeping the dogs, explaining to our supporters that the dogs had been refused entry to Australia.

This was an epic.

I rested my pounding head in my hands. I had forgotten that the newspaper following the story in Australia had been planning a feature on the two dogs returning to Australia and, of course, had wanted to focus on them being reunited with AJ's Nathan, and Danielle.

Depression sunk in as I realised I now had to let both of them know this turn of events too. With Christmas just around the corner, it was not going to be very festive news. What the hell were we going to do with the two dogs now? It was too late in the day to find foster homes. It was three days until Christmas. I wiped my eyes. This was just too much stress.

I rang Melissa again. We needed to cancel the planned flights. I just hoped we didn't lose the deposit. As I stood up from my desk, I sent a brief text message to Louise out in Afghanistan, so that she knew what was going on.

The simple 'Shit' texted back confirmed that she understood, and I reflected that if I knew Louise as well as I thought I did, then she was also now looking for an Australian to punch. And probably would too, if she found one.

I needed somewhere to put both dogs while we figured out this mess. In the past, I would have automatically taken one of the dogs in myself, but my one-bedroomed cottage on the outskirts of Liskeard barely had enough room for me and all my worldly possessions, let alone Nowzad, Tali and of course the nut-job dog known as Maxchat. Plus Hannah was due to travel down and stay over the festive period so, all in all, the inn was already very much full.

No, we were going to have to shell out some more charity money and put the dogs into kennels until we could come up with a new plan.

I picked up my mobile from my desk and dialled the number for Drum Kennels, an isolated facility on the outskirts of Honiton with glorious views out towards the Jurassic Coast. Morag and her husband, John, ran the kennels as a family enterprise and were all too familiar with the work of the charity. In the past, when I had needed to travel either for my own business or on behalf of the charity, Nowzad and the gang had been booked in for their own holidays.

All four dogs always almost ripped my arm off on the short walk down the narrow road from the parking spot to the boarding kennel reception, crazily wagging their tails – or stump, in the case of Nowzad – as they excitedly rushed to greet Morag. I had no idea how many treats they must have received during their stays, but something fired them up when they knew where we were going.

Morag listened intently to my brief and very to the point conversation about the officials in Australia and their new policies – my choice words giving her a fair indication of my current feelings towards those in charge of the policy – and the predicament we now found ourselves in with the dogs.

'No problem, Pen. Just bring them over when you can,' Morag replied straightaway, as I finished my ranted explanation.

We had assumed that their stay with Morag would be for a few months at the most while we sorted out new blood tests and then the flights, and booked Australian quarantine.

Ohhh . . . just how wrong could we have been?

chapter 22

All Hail, Cesar

The crowd of around 7,000 people, crammed into the Cardiff Arena, was enjoying the show. Cesar Millan, the famed dog trainer from California, with his own TV show and many books describing his unique method of talking to dogs was, to most of the eager fans hoping to pick up tips, just a tiny figure centre stage. But the enormous digital screens erected on either side of the platform gave them all an improved view of proceedings.

Sarah had travelled the two hours by car to Wales that March 2010 with her friend, Pippa, all the way from Yeovil, especially to watch the great dog man himself. Not really knowing what to expect, it had turned out to be a fun show: the colourful character that was Cesar was extremely entertaining as a live act, and he kept the crowd enthralled with demonstrations of calming techniques on randomly owned local dogs that had only been selected to come on stage just a few hours earlier, all claiming to have huge behavioural problems that only the dog whisperer himself could fix.

Sarah had also been happily impressed with one of the

'support acts' (as she called it): a bloke called Pen who ran an animal charity in Afghanistan.

Appearing on stage with a supporting video playing on the big screens, and a large dog in tow – the breed of which she had never heard of before – Pen had chatted to Cesar on stage as if they were just two guys in the pub about the epic trials of trying to deliver animal welfare in a country like Afghanistan.

'Wow, that sounds interesting,' Sarah had thought to herself. 'Maybe I can find out more about what they do.' It was an idea that had sparkled for a few seconds before she had promptly forgotten all about the bloke called Pen and his big white dog called Patchdog.

But it was March, the month of dog events culminating in Crufts, purported to be the biggest dog show in the world. Five cavernous halls of the National Exhibition Centre near Birmingham were taken over for a four-day period, with hundreds of judged events for every single breed of dog recognised by the Kennel Club.

The halls were, as usual, transformed into a massive dog lover's paradise with every dog-orientated piece of merchandise you could ever dream of being sold by the hundreds of trade stands that filled the gaps between the artificial grass arenas that were surrounded by row upon row of plastic chairs.

Fresh from the trip to see Cesar, Sarah recognised the name 'Nowzad Dogs' from the support act at the show in Cardiff immediately.

'Hey, look, it's that bloke from the Cesar thing.' She nudged Pippa to make her aware of the former soldier, who was in deep conversation with an interested member of the public. Behind him, pictures of dogs happily posing for the camera against a backdrop of sand and weaponry from Afghanistan lined the back wall of the charity trade stand that he was manning. The table in front of him was overflowing with branded charity merchandise, obviously designed to tempt the public and bring in the funds.

Curious to find out more, Sarah hovered at the table, letting her fingers browse through the pens, mugs and key rings with photos of soldiers and their beloved four-legged companions, before the dramatic and cute front-cover picture of three young pups standing in front of an olive-green door grabbed her attention. *One Dog at a Time*: *Saving the Strays of Helmand* read the book's title.

'Hmm, looks interesting,' Sarah thought to herself. Paying for a copy, she placed it in her bag, ready to start reading on her way home.

The book did indeed turn out to be an interesting read – sad in places, yet heartfelt and intriguing all at the same time . . . Reading it reignited Sarah's previous thoughts about wanting to know more about the charity but that thought, too, lasted just a brief moment before, finally putting the book down, she once more forgot about the bloke called Pen and his dogs in Afghanistan. Leaving the book's story, she had returned to the real world to be immersed in her everyday life with her best friends, Milo and Ben.

Ben, a collie cross, had been rescued to fill the void left by the sad demise of Sam.

Over a year later, as Sarah barged and shoved her way through the crowds mingling along the trade stands of Hall One at Crufts, she found herself once more in front of the

Nowzad Dogs stand. Remembering her forgotten promises to find out more about what the charity, Sarah popped some small change in the yellow charity tin on the cluttered stand, said hello to Pen and left with a bright coloured charity information leaflet clutched in her hand.

Back home, as the dark nights gave her and the dogs a not-really-needed excuse to stay in, Sarah explored the charity's website and the many stories of soldiers and their rescued companions. The tales of devotion to an abandoned cat or dog on the front lines of Afghanistan were both moving and fascinating: Sarah had never imagined that animal rescue on this scale would be able to function in a war-torn country like Afghanistan. The only reports she had ever heard from Afghanistan were on the six o'clock news and normally involved the sad news that another British serviceman had been killed or injured.

The story of Brin, a short-legged, dark tan dog really grabbed her attention.

In the wild lands of Helmand Province Brin, who had been found starving and alone, had been adopted by lads from the British Army manning a nearby patrol base. Although they were banned from keeping the sociable dog, they had discovered that, when he accompanied the soldiers on patrols, he had a natural talent for sniffing out danger.

Two British soldiers can rightly say they owe their lives to the super-sensitive nose that warned them of a buried bomb.

The stray canine knew his patch and knew that something was amiss. His constant barking towards one spot of freshly turned dirt had alerted the troops to bring in the mine detection equipment, revealing a bomb that would have killed the two soldiers who had been unaware of its presence as they approached it.

Nor did Brin's story end there. In an attack carried out by the Taliban on a British position, the troop's favourite four-legged companion was captured and held prisoner. Military protocol and orders prevented any form of rescue effort being launched. Afghan Special Forces, however, hot on the heels of the Taliban commander who had planned the raid, found and recognised Brin when they stormed the Taliban camp.

Returned to the grateful British soldiers, Brin's ordeal was far from over. With an imminent order to withdraw from the area, the soldiers knew that Brin would be left behind to once more fend for himself – something they couldn't contemplate.

Nowzad Dogs had been alerted to the plight of the hero dog from Helmand by Sally, a friend of one of the soldiers caring for Brin. An international fundraising campaign had been quickly initiated to gather the funds necessary to see Brin transported from Afghanistan to England, and the six months of quarantine he would need.

Sally even sold her car to help meet the funding target to get the dog out of Dodge. Quoted in a national newspaper to explain her reasons for going all-out to rescue Brin, she said: 'He had been through so much but this never stopped him being loyal, loving and brave. Despite being left starving and abandoned, he found new humans to love and saved the soldiers' lives and has made the most loving pet. He is one in a million.'

Sarah felt real empathy for the story of Brin and, through Facebook, became extremely good friends with Sally and the rest of the hardcore Nowzad crew who posted and called for fundraising to support the charity's work at every opportunity. Sarah found she fitted in with the ethos of the supporters' network immediately, and volunteered to help on the Nowzad Dogs stand the following year at Crufts.

It was a decision that would completely change her life.

chapter 23

Couldn't Make It Up

You couldn't make it up.

'Seriously, Melissa, you couldn't make this up.' I wanted to bang my head against the office wall. Slowly, repetitively and very hard.

From the look on her face, Melissa was probably not far from taking that drastic course of action herself. In fact, there was a lovely blank section of wall right there in our very bare office. I edged closer to it so I could get in first.

'Unbelievable.' I wanted to cry. 'So let me get this straight,' I started. It was getting surreal and very complicated. 'Wylie ad AJ survive against the odds in Afghanistan but can't freaking get out of England?' This truly was excruciatingly painful.

Melissa was probably more annoyed than me; she was just better at concealing it.

'Yup,' was all she replied.

I took a deep breath. I needed to calm down.

When the dogs had finished their first six months of quarantine we had moved them to Drum Kennels, which was a darn sight cheaper than quarantine for a start, plus it was friendlier. Morag ensured that all the dogs in her care were taken out into an exercise yard each day but, more importantly, when we visited them, we could actually take them out for a walk as neither was under the restrictive rules of quarantine. They had passed the rabies entry test as far as the United Kingdom was concerned.

Taking them out for the first time was an interesting experience, however. The boarding kennels was situated on the steep-sided slope of a hill that eventually fell away into Sidmouth. The single lane was narrow even for one car, and left no room to avoid passing vehicles unless you were nimble enough to climb up onto the verge and into the hedgerow as the car squeezed passed. Which made it a right barrel of laughs when you had a large Kuchi dog called AJ in tow, who was not really too keen on the lead and collar game.

As luck would have it, more or less every time I dropped off my pack for their brief stays with Morag, I never encountered any traffic in that lane as the five of us sprinted hell-for-leather to meet Morag at the front gate, the faded brass bell hanging there for visitors to announce themselves pretty irrelevant when my lot turned up.

However, typically, when Hannah and I first ventured only 100 yards or so down the lane with Wylie and AJ, both of us desperately pulling on their leads to try and slow the two madly straining dogs, from behind us the dreaded sound of an approaching car signalled we had a problem.

Both dogs ignored the rapidly closing engine noise as they sniffed the grassy verge for all they were worth, before bolting off another few yards to start the process all over again.

'There is never a car on this lane!' I shouted, the only solution geeing the dogs up to do their sprinting thing again, and desperately trying to stay on our feet as they dragged us down the hill at breakneck speed until we could jump off the road and into the safety of a passing bay.

AJ by now had become a bit of a beast. He had been large as a puppy, and he was even larger as an adolescent dog. Friendly and lovable, though, but as strong as an ox. Being cooped up for most of the day didn't help when he finally did have the option to stretch his legs.

Wylie, too, was just so fast on his feet. As soon as the boarding kennel gated run was opened he wanted to be off. The lead had to be around his neck prior to any inkling of the gate being opened to the outside world.

But both dogs seemed happy and that was the main thing. And they were both particularly happy that they had managed to bring a good friend over to the kennels with them from their time in quarantine.

Grandma Rose wasn't really their grandma, but she had picked up the nickname from her delightful online relation-ship with two of the Nowzad team, Sally and Sue. Sally, of course, had Brin, and Sue had Kilo, an energetic Afghan rescue that her daughter, serving in Helmand, had struck up a friendship with when she found the abandoned pup and decided to care for him during her tour of duty.

With both dogs having an online presence, Rose had morphed into Grandma Rose to the both of them, and her close locality to the quarantine facilities had seen her straight away volunteer her services to visit the two of them every single week to keep them company – alongside her already busy commitment of running the charity's eBay page.

When I had informed Rose that both dogs were going to Drum and the reasons why, she had once more stepped in to volunteer to continue visiting with both dogs. Once again, I had reflected on how glad I was that we had her on-board with us.

But, once more, an unexpected turn of events had completely scuppered our plans.

Under the new guidelines for entry into Australia so we could be issued with the all-important import certificate, both dogs had been required to pass a raft of blood tests. We had thought it was just a formality.

It wasn't.

AJ failed the rabies blood test. It didn't mean he had rabies; it just meant he didn't have a high enough antibody count as required by Australia.

In turn, Wylie passed the rabies test but failed the leishmaniasis test, again not meeting the required standard that Australia now demanded from dogs arriving from the United Kingdom.

The United Kingdom itself didn't call for a leishmaniasis test to be carried out for entry. It was complicated stuff.

'So,' I continued now with Melissa, as I thought I had the facts straight, 'we have to revaccinate both of them, wait thirty days and then resubmit them both for expensive blood tests again, and *then* go through this whole one hundred and fifty days waiting game *again*?'

Once again, Melissa was direct and to the point as she sat in her office chair waiting patiently for me to finish stating what was clearly obvious to her.

'Yup.'

To say I swore was an understatement. The walls of the white, windowless office echoed with profanities as I vented at the cost that the charity have to fork out. The dogs had failed their blood tests; it was that simple. Nobody could have seen that one coming.

And I knew without a doubt that Nathan and Danielle were not going to be best pleased.

They weren't.

And I got the subtle impression from the tone of their emails that somehow they thought that we, as a charity, could have done more. But there was nothing more we could rightly do.

I had to consider the negative impact it would have on our supporters if I continued to ask for funding to support the two dogs. We had just enough money in the kitty. I decided I would explain briefly to our supporters about the blood-test situation, as they were desperate for news of the two dogs, and then we would just have to suck it up and start the taxing process all over again.

chapter 24

Meeting Wylie

During her stint at Crufts during March 2012, wearing her tan Nowzad Dogs volunteer T-shirt, Sarah had attempted to sell the work of the charity to unsuspecting show visitors as they strolled passed the charity's stall.

While most were obviously more interested in spending their cash on something from the many commercial stands to take home for their own, very loved, four-legged companion than on a wayward street dog in Afghanistan they had never met, after a day or so of watching the crowds, Sarah had begun to appreciate who was genuinely interested and could, most of the time, spot the ones who would feasibly donate if the tin was rattled loud enough.

It didn't stop her being taken aback by some when she completely misjudged their character, however: 'Do you pay staff wages?' she had been asked in a scolding kind of way by a particularly dishevelled-looking older woman in a plain brown raincoat.

'Well, yes,' Sarah had replied, without thinking too hard about her answer. After all, she guessed that at least the Afghan staff at the Nowzad shelter would be paid.

'Then I am not donating,' the woman curtly replied, without hesitation. 'I only donate to charities that are made up of volunteers.' And that was that.

Sarah wasn't entirely sure, but rightly assumed that no Afghans were going to volunteer to pick up dog poo.

Before she could argue the point with the abrupt woman, the lady had already turned away – clutching a charity pencil that she hadn't paid for – before scurrying off to presumably annoy somebody else.

The pencil was but a small sacrifice.

I had been on the stand as well for a few days, playing the role of founder and chatting to as many people as possible when they took an interest in the charity's wares for sale.

Striking up a conversation with me during one of the quieter moments, Sarah had realised that the legendary Wylie, who now had a Facebook page of his own, was being looked after at a boarding kennels near to Honiton. That being only a 45-minute drive away from her cottage in Yeovil, the beginnings of an idea formed.

Sarah had thought she was being incredibly forward to ask if she could visit that legend of a dog, and she was slightly stunned when I agreed immediately to her visiting Wylie, even suggesting she could take the crazy little fella out for a walk!

That was way more than she had hoped for! In fact, it would be amazing. She was going to actually meet one of the fabled mutts of the Nowzad Dogs hall of fame.

Sarah had been incredibly disappointed when I had failed to turn up at a talk a few months previously. Not because she was desperate to listen to my presentation about Afghanistan and the work at the shelter, but because Nowzad, the original dog of the charity, had been tagging along with me.

Breaking down on the M5 and being towed back to Exeter had not been a good enough excuse in Sarah's book. She had been really intrigued to meet the dog that had started everything. Having read about the exploits to save the cropped-eared fighting dog, the opportunity to meet the dog in person had not been one to be missed.

But now that I had given her the opportunity to meet Wylie, she forgave me.

Crufts could not go quickly enough as she planned her first visit to the kennels.

Sarah's underlying mission was to meet Wylie in person and apologise to him for the way 'man' had treated him. Sarah felt that Wylie had been so let down by mankind. She wanted to make it up to him. And visiting him in kennels and showing him companionship seemed like a good place to start.

A slight communication problem followed as Sarah turned up to visit Wylie and AJ but nobody at the kennels knew who she was and were reluctant to let her anywhere near their star guests.

I had forgot to inform Morag of Sarah's impending arrival.

'And this guy runs the charity?' Sarah had thought to herself as she waited for phone calls to be made that would confirm who she was.

Everything sorted out, Wylie had turned out to be the fluffballed little monster that she had imagined him to be. The former street dog went crazy the first time she had been allowed into his boarding kennel run, and he greeted her as if he had known her his whole life. His short tail had wagged so fast as he ran and danced around her, not stopping still long enough for her to make any sort of fuss of him before he scooted off then turned to dart nimbly between her legs.

Arranging to meet Grandma Rose and her husband, Nigel, who Sarah had heard lots about via the Facebook crowd but never actually met, was her ticket to being allowed to take Wylie and AJ out for a walk in the lanes surrounding the boarding facility.

Immediately upon meeting Rose, Sarah knew it was the start of a great friendship, and their weekly get-together became a regular opportunity for the two of them to shower the captive dogs with love and affection until they were calm enough to slip a lead over their necks and attempt the dog walk thing.

No matter how many times they visited, both dogs would spend the first few minutes of each visit in hype mode, as if they had never been visited before. It was heart-breaking to leave them after what seemed like an all too brief visit, but that was the way it had to be.

Sarah could understand my reluctance to foster the dogs out. Both were determined to experience freedom and with the attention on all the various social media platforms that Wylie attracted more or less daily, she could see that I couldn't risk a careless moment from a foster carer, like a door being left slightly open and the charity's star rescue running off.

Explaining that would be an epic.

No, the boarding kennels probably was the best place to ensure the charity met its responsibilities to take care of Wylie and AJ until they could fly to Australia.

As the days began to draw closer to the impending date of Wylie and AJ's October flight neared after all the months of revaccinations and blood tests, Rose and Sarah began to feel the pangs of sadness stabbing away each time they brought the dogs back into the kennels at the end of their time walking them. Both ladies knew that the day would come when they brought them back and then would never see either dog again.

And for Rose the last time she was to walk Wylie at the boarding kennels was sooner than she had planned. As always during the initial few minutes of a walk, Wylie would pull like a steam train in his excitement to be out and sniffing the real world, rather than the disinfected kennel world that he occupied for the majority of every day.

Rose hadn't expected the sudden yank on the lead from Wylie as he dramatically decided he should be going in the other direction. Her feet were not quite in the right position to maintain her balance and over she went.

At least the break was clean, but she wouldn't be walking a boisterous dog again. Her ankle would not have healed until long after both had flown the coop.

The depressing day – the last time they could visit either dog at Drum Kennels – arrived. Sarah accompanied Rose and Nigel so that Rose could stay in the car, her ankle in a cast, eagerly waiting as Sarah led each dog up the steep hill for their final goodbyes with their Grandma Rose.

Tears all round, it was a sad few moments. Both dogs looked confused. Clearly they had no idea what all the fuss was about.

It was heart-breaking. With just days to go before both dogs were due to fly we had received the worst news possible.

There was really was not a lot we could say to each other. Melissa looked as if she was about to cry and I probably didn't look very far from it. Inside I was a bag of raw emotions, mainly anger, but frustration and disappointment bubbled away too, alongside each other.

The brief and to the point email from the quarantine station had been brutal. Their bedside manner left a lot to be desired.

As you may know, leishmaniasis is endemic in Afghanistan in both the human and the dog populations. In dogs, it can take a range of courses from very mild and transient to severe, resulting in death. It has a long incubation period of 3 months to 7 years, which might explain why Wylie has tested positive now. The disease is exotic to Australia.

This is really disappointing given what has gone into the care and preparation of Wylie over the last 18 months.

'Disappointing!?' I screamed at the office wall. 'They just say "really disappointing"?' It was actually the worst thing that could have happened! 'It's bloody *unbelievable* after all *we*'ve put into the time and effort into trying to get him to Australia!'

To be honest, it had been Melissa getting up in the middle of the night to make the phone calls to the quarantine facility, ending up playing telephone tennis with staff on the other end of the line who were unable to answer questions about issues we were clearly meant to understand, but they needed to put to an experienced vet.

But that was it: Wylie wasn't going to start a new life in Australia. He was staying put.

AJ, though, had passed all the tests this time and the issued import certificate cleared him to fly. I collected him from a sad Morag for the long drive to Heathrow. Morag had realised she would never actually see the big dope again – it was quite depressing as I, too, realised that the big man had finally earned his flight Down Under. I would miss him. He was the proverbial gentle giant.

His last walk on English soil was around the grass verges of Fleet Services along the M3 motorway. I was conscious of losing him after all we had been through to get him this far, but the heavy-set dog just wanted to have a wee and stretch his legs, and I was happy to oblige him.

I delivered him to a company called Airpets who arranged the travel for companion animals heading to far-flung countries. Kelly, the pet export travel consultant, greeted me and AJ at their staging facility and instantly fell in love with the big dog.

After a sad, final cuddle with the big man, I said my last goodbyes.

Nothing else could go wrong.

But it did, of course. On the morning of AJ's planned flight, Melissa received a call from Kelly at Airpets informing us that AJ's move to Australia was being delayed for 24 hours.

Melissa asked, 'Why?' already dreading the answer she was about to get back.

The simple explanation was forthcoming: they needed a new Sky Kennel. AJ had chewed his way out of his original one while sitting in the flight line to be loaded on to the cargo section of the aircraft.

AJ and Nathan would finally, after nearly eighteen months, be successfully reunited in October 2012. The stressful phone calls and emails were instantly forgotten as he saw the dog he had rescued as a pup looking out at him from the quarantine kennel AJ was currently occupying in the Australian quarantine station.

To cap it all with the depressing Wylie saga, Danielle and I had lost direct contact. I had emailed her constantly to keep her informed, but hadn't had a reply. The quarantine station commander in Australia was apparently in communication with her, and was relaying the proceedings as they happened.

I emailed the Australian police force HQ to try and find her. I was told she had been on some form of training exercise without access to communication.

What could I do? I had had enough. Wylie most definitely had had enough.

'Right, decision made,' I stated, a calmness suddenly suffusing through me as I realised the way ahead for Wylie.

'Who could we foster Wylie out to?' I asked Melissa, as she stared into her empty coffee cup.

Brainstorming the potential candidates wasn't too difficult as the list wasn't that long.

Much like Louise when she had applied for the job at the Nowzad Dogs shelter all those years ago, there was only one person on the list.

Sarah was surprised to take the call from Melissa at the Nowzad Dogs office.

The phone call was brief and to the point. Sarah was actually quite shocked at first. Then pleased and then shocked again. And she of course said yes. Which left her with another problem. But it was all good. She could make it work, she guessed. Hoped. 'Oh, crap,' was another of the random thoughts that flashed through her brain during the brief phone call.

Melissa had broken the news that Wylie was not going to be flying to Australia. Ever.

And had asked if Sarah would consider fostering the lovable but now constantly unlucky mutt.

It was a foregone conclusion Sarah would say yes.

But Sarah was already thinking about her landlady, what would she say? Sarah knew she had to be careful. Her cottage was rented, and the terms of her lease stated she could only have two dogs, and she already had Ben and Milo. Her landlady lived on site too, just opposite in fact, in the grand old farmhouse that overlooked her homely little cottage. Would she say yes to a third dog? She would have to soft soap somewhat. But Sarah knew she was good at that, so all good there.

Her landlady would say yes, wouldn't she?

Sarah collected Wylie from Morag. He had been in the kennels for nearly ten months. Whilst it was fantastic he was finally going to a loving home with somebody he clearly loved too, the staff were of course sad to see him leave. He was one of their own. Wylie had become part of their routine. But it was time. Just like AJ, he needed a new adventure.

Taking him home had been a precisely planned event that Sarah was quite proud of. Her boss, Bruce, himself a dog lover, had even been arm-twisted into assisting. After all, when she took days away with her circle of friends, it was Bruce who kindly offered his services to be on hand to be her dog sitter for Milo and Ben. Bruce had even turned his hand to baking tasty dog treats, which the charity had sold during the previous Crufts. He thoroughly enjoyed taking charge of the dogs and was happy to be a part of the Wylie introduction plan.

The scenic Ham Hill country park sits majestically south of the A303. It is a lovely place to take dogs for a walk through forested tracks and open fields that always lead you back to the dog-friendly Prince of Wales pub. A winner whichever way you looked at it.

Sarah had planned it so that Wylie and her two dogs Ben and Milo would all meet on neutral territory – Bruce brought her two dogs along as Sarah arrived with Wylie.

The meet and greet thankfully went as planned: each dog took it in turns to sniff the others' bums before they returned to sniffing the surrounding grass.

Sarah looked at Bruce, who returned the questioning stare. Both had secretly been expecting a fight of sorts to break out.

It hadn't.

The meet had been a complete anti-climax.

When they arrived home later in the day to her farm cottage, all three dogs more or less walked into the house as if they had always lived there together. Sarah knew her original two dogs were accommodating but this was ridiculous. It was like they were saying, 'Come on in, Wylie!'

'Hey, cheers, Milo and Ben. Don't mind if I do!'

Sarah was looking for Wylie. He wasn't on the floor in or by the dog bed that he favoured. Nor was he on the floor in the kitchen or in the hallway to the sitting room.

Ben and Milo looked at her knowingly.

Sarah was curious. Neither dog ever looked at her like that. They knew something she didn't.

And that, she knew, was the whereabouts of Wylie.

Her two veteran dogs just looked at her: 'For crying out loud, boss, it's obvious where the idiot boy is!' was what they were trying to tell her.

The fluffy tail as it wagged slightly from its drooped position hanging over the edge of the kitchen table gave the game away. Unbelieving, Sarah looked up to see Wylie, cool as a cucumber, sitting on the kitchen table. Just sitting there. Like it was the most natural place in the world for a dog to be.

Sarah shook her head in complete shock. 'Wylliiieeeeeee!'

The Afghan mutt who had been to hell and back slowly got off the table.

Sarah had thought Milo was friendly and boisterous, always dragging Ben around in a playful way or dragging Sarah over with him to meet a new dog on their patch. At times, Sarah had thought Milo's antics extremely annoying.

But then she had taken Wylie home.

Wylie had the ability to make Milo look like he was a sloth when it came to play time. He was a menace, but in a good way. With limited social skills, a fact that was easy to excuse given where he had come from, Wylie had no idea of when it was time to stop his overzealous playful attitude. Nibbling ears and tails was his favourite. Especially with Ben. The collie, fast asleep upside down on the sofa, would suddenly find his long, beautiful tail being used as a tug toy. Which of course Ben was not too amused about.

Mr Playful was coming out of his shell. It had taken a long time for Wylie to trust people which, at first, Sarah had found slightly upsetting as Wylie would seem happy and contented but reluctant to be actively engaged in direct play with her. But, as time went on, she realised he was finding his feet and needed to adjust to the new world he had suddenly found himself in. One where one person was a constant and could be trusted. After all, he had been through so much. Nobody could blame the unconfident dog if he took his time.

Out for walks, Wylie was more or less fairly cool with other dogs – unless, of course, they got in his face. Sarah would look towards the heavens when, with Wylie *clearly* on his lead, they approached an unfamiliar dog owner who failed to take control of their own wandering dog. The ensuing dance of Sarah and Wylie as he tried to either escape the attentions of the off-lead dog or worse, went snapping for the other dog as Sarah desperately tried to drag him away – which was almost impossible due to the other dog continuing its close-quarter antagonistic tactics – was beyond frustrating.

But, all things considered, Wylie was just a good lad. And Sarah loved him to bits.

She also knew what she was going to do with him.

Deep down, she knew that together they could win it. Wylie was the perfect candidate for her to enter Scruffts with. With the epic tale that Wylie came with, nobody in the ring could better him. Well, she hoped they wouldn't anyway. It would just be a fantastic opportunity for the charity she now loved to receive some brilliant PR.

Her only doubt was to whether the organisers would be happy for her to win the competition for a second time. But, 'Who cares?' she had said definitely to a fast-asleep Wylie, his back legs kicking out as he dreamt. Sarah hoped it was a good dream and that Wylie was chasing something, and not the other way around.

No, she would worry about what any concerns the organisers had when and if she got that far.

chapter 25

Dog Showtastic

'Yeah, we can go to London in the car. It'll be fine,' Sarah said as she looked over at Wylie, who was, once again, sitting upright like a Sphinx guarding a pharaoh's tomb, on the wooden kitchen table, as if that was what every dog was meant to do. 'Afghan, get off the bloody table!' Sarah scolded him.

For reasons unknown, Sarah had a bizarre habit of calling Wylie something other than his given name. He had now progressed from Herbert to Afghan, just as Ben the quiet collie had become Super Ken. It was a weird habit that Sarah adopted from time to time.

'I need to remember to call you Wylie in public,' Sarah said out loud, reminding herself, as Wylie/Afghan removed himself from the table and reluctantly trotted over to lie next to Milo in a vacant dog bed on the floor.

The first heat for the 2014 Scruffts was being held during the London Pet Show in May 2013; Sarah had applied and been successful. Entry box ticked.

Held in the gigantic halls of Earls Court, it was a two-day pet-lover's fest of every animal imaginable being shown off in an attempt to entice new pet owners into the fold. If you are debating the idea of having a pet, then the London Pet Show is all about responsible pet ownership, and you can't fault the organisers for that.

Wylie wasn't a seasoned car traveller, but plonking him in the back of the car on a dog bed, with the dog guard separating him from the back seats, caused no problems. The gentle dog seemed cool with it.

Sarah took the same route as she had with Milo during his rise to fame back in 2011. Parking her car at Richmond Station, on the outskirts of London, she knew it would be a simple case of walking Wylie, who by now had grown accustomed to not pulling when on a lead as he had finally realised he was getting a walk either way, onto the platform and to then hop onto the train.

Wylie enjoyed the short ride on the train, sitting quietly by Sarah's feet as the bustle of London's commuter scene hustled by, mostly unaware of the four-legged passenger sharing their world.

Staying at a dog-friendly hotel in Hammersmith, Wylie behaved as if he was back at the Yeovil cottage – although jumping onto the bed to snuggle next to Sarah was a rare treat, and one that she wasn't going to begrudge him.

Next morning a new experience awaited them. With both the District and Circle underground lines going from Hammersmith to Earls Court, Sarah jumped on the first train that approached. There followed a short trip on the clacking Tube train, which Wylie seemed unfazed at before they alighted at Earls Court and were immediately confronted with an escalator.

Oops!

She must have jumped on the Circle line train that runs

deeper underground and instead of easy to manage steps they had installed an escalator up to street level.

With Milo she must have come on the District line which only has steps and was therefore easy to negotiate with a dog in tow.

The Transport for London policy is that whilst all dogs are more than welcome to travel on the Tube – especially as most behave better than some of the underground's human clientele – they must be carried on escalators.

Sarah looked around. It was a fair policy for the majority of Londoners who owned a handbag-sized dog as was the fashion driven by celebs like Paris Hilton, but not for those who owned a formerly abused rescue dog from Afghanistan who weighed almost twenty kilos.

She had never picked him up before. Would he freak out? Struggle?

She had no idea what was about to happen. But they had to get there, and as she couldn't afford the black cab ride, what would be, would be.

Sarah hefted the unsuspecting dog up into her arms like a baby, then carefully stepped onto the bottom step of the escalator.

Wylie, to his credit, just lolled in Sarah's arms, watching the passengers on the descending escalator doing double-takes and pointing as Sarah looked straight ahead as if carrying a dog up the escalator was the most natural thing in the world.

Once out of the tube and on the street, Wylie sniffed like crazy at all the new smells on the London street. Sarah took a firmer grip on his lead. Wylie had a big day ahead of him.

The packed audience for the Scruffts heat during the pet show loved the heartbreaking tale of Wylie's tough former life. The organisers for the year had introduced two new classes for the 2014 competition, which Sarah had realised were in Wylie's favour. Milo had originally won 'Most Handsome' which, for Wylie, probably wasn't his best asset. But this year had seen the introduction, alongside the new 'Good Citizen' category, of 'Best Crossbreed Rescue'.

Sarah was one excited Somerset girl. Without a doubt Wylie was a crossbreed, although of which two types of dog was anyone's guess; and he most definitely had outstanding credentials as a rescued dog.

Sarah had not been prepared for the microphone that was thrust in her face as she stood in the ring waiting for the judges' inspection. She hadn't realised the owners would be expected to explain their dog's story to the expectant crowd. Live. Wearing her Nowzad T-shirt had been the limit of her anticipated promotion for the charity as she had assumed that the announcer would read out Wylie's story.

At first Sarah struggled to think of what to say.

The crowd was poised and silent as she flipped mentally through Wylie's story and what she could say about the life that he had survived to lead him there survived to lead him there.

'Well,' she began, 'I guess the first thing to say about Wylie is that despite his horrendous start in life, which saw him starving, beaten and his ears being cut off, he is the one of the most gentle dogs I know.' Unrehearsed, she knew she was starting hesitantly but, as she told his story she warmed to the task, the crowd began to cheer and clap and, by the time she had finished talking, the crowd was on its feet. Overcome with emotion at the enthusiastic approval of the audience, Sarah realised that she had done the unassuming dog from Kandahar proud.

With her mum and Pippa on hand to give out the limited supply of the Nowzad Dogs leaflets she had brought with her, Sarah and Wylie were mobbed afterwards by folk wanting to meet the brave little dog.

He had won outright, and Wylie was through to the semifinals of Scruffts best crossbreed rescue later in the year.

The journey home, however, was not the uneventful trip Sarah had assumed it would be. Elation from the win was instantly forgotten as Wylie decided, as they sped along the A303 towards home, that he now didn't particularly enjoy long car journeys. Whining and scratching away in the back of the car, Sarah had to stop at every opportunity to attempt to calm him before reluctantly scooping him back into the car, only to repeat the process half an hour later down the road.

Both she and Wylie had been extremely relieved to see the welcoming, waggy tails of Ben and Milo as they had finally pulled up at the end of the mud-tracked road that led to home. Long car journeys were now, for some reason, not Wylie's cup of tea.

With his blue jeans, blue T-shirt, brown field boots and black cowboy hat, you could have been mistaken for thinking that he was actually in character for a role that was being secretly filmed; the cameras and director hidden away in the towering trees that stood guard at the edge of the field.

But he wasn't in character. He was just being himself.

TV actor Martin Clunes looked relaxed, his trademark grin greeting all as he strolled between the gazeboes and tents that made up the event, shaking hands and chatting away to visitors and entrants alike. Spectators lined the temporarily erected wooden fences that denoted the arenas where the rescued dogs were being judged.

Now and again he was reminded of his forthcoming judging duties, which he knew was an immense responsibility, but one he had gladly accepted. In his programme notes, Martin had emphasised just how impossible it would be to choose a winner from all the deserving rescues that had entered as, in his eyes, they were all winners.

Martin and his wife, Philippa, had first tried the format for the fair in 2008 on a plot of land they had brought near to their farm in Beaminster, Dorset. Bizarrely, as without knowing it when the land had been purchased, it came with an ancient charter bestowing the holder of the land permission to hold a fair each year.

With his wife sharing his passion for horses and dogs, they had decided to open up the land to hold the Buckham Fair which, as the popularity of it grew year after year, now included many different rescue-dog classes, along with entertaining displays by police dogs and vintage cars, to name but a few of the attractions throughout the day. And it didn't stop there – trade stands and even an indoor deli selling local produce came on board to tempt all who supported the day.

Martin could be justly proud, as the fair had raised thousands of pounds for local charities and was becoming a must-attend event throughout the south-west. But for those who managed to be selected with their rescue dogs via the qualifying show in Dorset, there was another incentive for going all-out to win the coveted title of overall champion of the Buckham Fair: the £350 that would be donated to the registered charity of the winner's choice. Sarah could think of no better way for Wylie to keep his 'paws in' so to speak in preparation for Scruffts and keep the Nowzad Dog's profile in the public eye.

Sarah smiled at Wylie as they waited their turn in the improvised ring in the middle of the field. She was wearing her brown Nowzad Dogs T-shirt despite the ominous rain clouds that were building overhead, as she was determined to promote the charity as best she could. She already knew that if Wylie won it would be a great cash boost for the charity. And, of course, as anyone who knew Sarah would know, she couldn't pass up the opportunity to enter a dog show.

After the unexpected mike that had been thrust into her face in front of hundreds of spectators during the heats at the London Pet Show, Sarah had come prepared, her now-practised patter weighed off and ready to go.

Once she let people know Wylie's heartbreaking story, she was confident it would be game, set and match.

She wasn't being big headed: facts were facts. What Wylie had been forced to survive back in the violent, harsh landscape of Kandahar was, at times, unbelievable and, without question, more devastating than any other rescue stories Sarah had come across. Even thinking back to her own little Ted, his adorably handsome Jack Russell face winning rescue show after rescue show as he had gained the sympathy of the judges . . . well, he had actually had it pretty easy.

No, Wylie was without doubt unique, and if any rescue dog was to be called deserving of the title then call her biased, but it was him. Having already been chosen through to the final by the preliminary Buckham Fair judging panel, she knew she had to convince the final judge and a celebrity one to boot. So as long as Mr Clunes was not made of too-stern stuff, then Sarah was willing to bet they had this.

Martin had not yet met the affectionate fluffball, Wylie, but he was about to. Going along the line of deserving rescue dogs, he listened intently as he was told their stories. There was Toby the terrier cross who was rescued as a stray in Ireland and brought over to the Margaret Green rescue centre near Tavistock. Timid and shy, he had come on by leaps and bounds with the care from his adopted family. Next to him was another Toby, also rescued from Ireland, who had almost died eating a packet of headache tablets but was saved and now enjoyed living in France. Then the elderly, black-coated Bonnie, rescued by the Labrador Trust, who had been bullied by her previous family's other dog. The line of rescues was long and, while all credit had to be given to the families who had adopted these once sad dogs from a lonely existence in a shelter, none could honestly compare to what Sarah's Wylie had been through.

The photo printed in the following week's *Western Gazette* painted the picture that told anybody all they needed to know: Martin stood casually in his cowboy hat, his left arm pulling Sarah tightly to him as she grinned happily whilst proudly displaying the red, white and blue long-tailed rosette, with Wylie patiently standing at her feet surveying his winner's domain.

Yet again, the darling dog of an Afghanistan rescue had wowed the crowd and, more importantly, the judges.

He just had to do it two more times.

chapter 26

Scruffts

The hype was beginning to build around the dog that had only just survived the treacherous streets of Kandahar, as word got out that Wylie had made it through to the semi-finals for the Scruffts competition, under the category of Best Crossbreed Rescue.

The event would, once again, be back at Earls Court in London but under the umbrella of the *Discover Dogs* show. Fittingly for Wylie, as it was soldiers who had first saved his life, it would be held on 11 November: Remembrance Day.

Sarah was slightly concerned about the amount of time off she was forced to ask for from her employer Bruce at Mole Valley Farmers to accommodate the press interviews that wanted to detail the exploits of the brave Afghan dog, but she need not have worried as Bruce, excited for her success, gave her the time off needed to stand in front of the cameras.

The local Somerset press had even called for the opportunity for a unique event: the two legends of Afghan rescue finally meeting face to face.

The setting of the rustic-looking farm courtyard was perfect. The day was hot and both dogs were panting heavily to keep themselves cool. Nowzad, the years show-ing on his war-scarred face, ears docked short against his tan-coloured head, eyed the young pretender carefully. Even struggling to walk, he could still surprise all with a sudden lunge if he saw a dog he didn't think should be in his space.

But on this occasion he just stared Wylie down. One bark. Just a gruff warning to tell the younger dog that, 'Hey, you might be the big thing around here now, but remember I started it all, laddie.'

Wylie, to his credit, just glanced casually back, both dogs showing a sort of mutual respect for the other.

They stood together long enough to have a photo taken. Both docked-eared, brothers in arms from their individual but shared stories of hardship and survival against the odds.

It was a unique moment.

Sarah had never considered that there would be this level of interest in either her or Wylie's story, but she knew that she was the one who had come up with the crazy idea of entering him for the show, so she sucked it up and talked to the many press outlets that were pestering to hear the 'tail'.

Her family and friends were incredibly supportive, and the online Nowzad community had really taken Wylie to heart, rallying behind Sarah and cheering her all the way. Some of their posts to the website read as if Wylie had already won the main event, such was the enthusiasm for 'Mr Wylster'.

Knowing full well that Wylie was probably not going to enjoy the journey in the car to London, Sarah had booked him a ticket on the train. Aware of his celebrity status and the packed nature of standard class, she booked in advance so they could travel in style in first class.

Wylie loved riding on the train and the underground. The main line from Yeovil took them all the way into Waterloo, which for Sarah meant the added burden of carrying Wylie up and down a whole host of escalators to make the various connections required to travel to Earls Court.

Wylie just took the whole journey in his stride. Whether sitting happily in the carriage of the train or riding the escalators in Sarah's arms, it seemed as if he thought it was just the thing that all dogs did.

Either way, it was one hell of a contrast from living under a rock in Afghanistan.

The show went pretty much as Sarah expected it to go. Wylie cracked on with being cute and adorable and loved the attention from the army of well-wishers that had flocked to support him.

The semi-finals of the other Scruffts crossbreed categories had already been held and the winners of each one were paraded around the ring, all safe in the knowledge that they were on their way to the grand final in March 2014.

But Wylie had still to jump that last hurdle.

Worried thoughts flooding through her mind. Would her previous success with Milo go against her? She nervously looked over at the judge, as if they had already discussed how dare she try and win the event again. Would she forget what to say? It was suddenly terrifying. A million times worse than with Milo.

Everybody knew who she was now. The media coverage

had been bonkers. The innocent young girl from Somerset who had started winning dog shows as a kid was now having her photo taken for national newspapers some twenty years later. It was surreal. The *Daily Mail* had just run a good half-page article on Wylie, his amazing story and Sarah's involvement. The newspaper editor had even liked the story so much that he had dispatched a photographer especially to stand guard over Sarah to snap the vital shot should Wylie actually win the semi-final. But what if they didn't win? Would there be a photo with her and Wylie standing dejectedly outside the hall, waiting for the tube home, splashed across the front pages?

Sarah felt the pressure mounting yet again as, suddenly, she found herself ushered into the arena along with the other semi-finalists of the crossbreed rescue category. After a quick parade, the mike was passed around so that each owner could talk about their crossbreed dog and why they felt it was worthy of winning the semi-final.

Sarah listened intently as each person told their tale. She couldn't help but look down at Wylie, his usual, oblivious expression unchanged as he waited patiently for the next dog biscuit that would be popped his way any time soon. Sarah was growing nervous.

But as the other finalist relayed their own 'tales' Sarah's confidence grew until finally she knew once more Wylie had it in the bag. Whilst all deserving to be in the ring none of the dogs had been through the horrors that Wylie had experienced. To coin a phrase, she was sure Wylie had blown the competition away. And if the noise of the crowd was anything to go by, they agreed, as Sarah took the mike and now fluently described the hardships and abuse that her beloved Wylie had endured to survive. As ever, she felt pretty emotional herself as she thought of the pain that he had gone through.

The judge stood off to one side to gather her thoughts before delivering the verdict.

She announced the third-placed dog. Sarah ignored it. It wasn't Wylie.

Second place was given out and, yet again, Wylie had not been called forward. Sarah thought, no, *knew*, he at least deserved a top-three finish.

The judge held the crowd for a few seconds longer . . .

'And the Scruffts Best Crossbreed Rescue dog of the year is . . . Wylie!'

Wylie had done it once again. The crowd was delighted.

Wylie and Sarah were now going to the grand finale of Scruffts at Crufts, the biggest dog show in the world.

'Wow thank you!' was all Sarah could think as the judge congratulated her.

Once more, Wylie was mobbed as they attempted to leave the show – complete strangers wanting to meet the hero dog from Afghanistan. Plus the self-proclaimed 'Nowzad crazies' were, as usual, lining up in their identical Nowzad T-shirts waiting to rush Sarah as she proudly held their rosette aloft for all to see.

Making it to the obscurity of London's underground network was actually somewhat of a relief.

Wylie and Sarah, her mum and Pippa jumped on the tube to start the journey home. Sarah headed for the empty end of the carriage to keep Wylie out of the way of the rushing commuters. The reason for the carriage's emptiness was apparent: an unwashed, downtrodden-looking tramp had pitched up for a ride around the tube, obviously to escape the cold November day. Sarah could instantly smell the alcohol.

But she wanted somewhere quiet for Wylie, and the tramp was doing a good job of creating a space on the fairly crowded tube. She sat down, still clutching the winner's rosette like it was an Olympic gold medal. Which in the world of dog rescue, it was.

The tramp's eyes lit up as soon as he saw Wylie sitting on the floor of the carriage. He stroked and talked to Wylie as they lurched from stop to stop along the dark tunnels of the tube. Wylie, Sarah could tell, liked the attention the tramp was giving him, too.

Due to the grime and weeks' old beard, Sarah couldn't figure out the guy's age. It was sad to think he had ended up like this. But the tramp seemed oblivious to his current predicament and was more interested to know why Wylie was on the train. Sarah summarised the story as quickly as she could: he had asked politely and was quite clearly interested, and she didn't want to arrive at Waterloo having only explained half the story.

The man was mesmerised by Wylie's life, perhaps comparing the similarities with his own homeless existence. His bedraggled and unkempt appearance was an indication to most that he was someone to be avoided – much like the Afghans had done to Wylie, never bothering to get to know the love the dog had for people.

Sarah found she really enjoyed talking to the vagrant guy for the brief period of their joint journey. At Waterloo, and leaving him alone to thoughts again, she felt sad. He had

actually seemed a pretty decent sort of chap, polite and cour-
teous, and she was thankful to Wylie for being the starting
point for the conversation that had followed.

The escalator to travel up to the surface of London and
the mainline station was long and steep and seemed to go
on for ever. Sarah was not only emotionally drained after
the stress of the semi-final, but she was knackered, too.
Heaving Wylie up into a carrying position on the front of
her chest, she stepped onto the slowly moving escalator.
Her mum and Pippa were unable to offer any help: both
were laden down with theirs and Sarah's overnight gear,
Wylie's stuff and the many dog-related bargains that they
had purchased from the show, which had been an inevitable consequence of the semi-finals being held in a dog
lovers' shopping paradise.

By the time they had reached the halfway point up the
escalator, Sarah didn't care that people were pointing and
waving at the carefree dog who by now had slipped down to
her waist. By the time they reached the top, commuters passing on the down escalator couldn't even see that she was
carrying a dog as her arms had slowly given out so much that
Wylie was now resting on her knees below the level of the
hand rail as they were both, thankfully, spewed safely over
the top and onto the station platform.

But, just as Sarah thought she could take it easy, Wylie
spied the station pigeons. It was a sight to behold as he
slipped and floundered on the smooth tiled floor of the
station as he tried desperately to pull away from her. She
thankfully had a firm hold on his lead. The pigeons
panicked and flew blindly towards unsuspecting commuters, who suddenly found themselves ducking to avoid a
pigeon face-plant.

In all, it had been a fantastic achievement. And, as if to underline this, all the replying to the many Facebook messages of support kept Sarah occupied for the long train ride home.

Christmas came and went without incident, the media interest in Wylie slowly fading as other stories took to the headlines.

Life seemed to fall back into normality as work and dog-walking blended into one, except for the addition of an extra face to her gang at the farm: Sarah's recently acquired fireman boyfriend, Ed. She had known him for a long time but never as boyfriend and girlfriend. Both had had unsuccessful relationships and that New Year's Eve had found Sarah alone with the dogs in her cottage. Chatting to Ed on Facebook had revealed that he, too, would be spending the evening alone. As friends, they thought they might as well see the New Year in together, at Sarah's place because of the dogs.

The cider had flowed and they'd nattered away about old times and places. Sarah was intrigued to see that Ed spent the majority of the evening cuddling Milo. Nobody cuddled Milo for too long as for a start, the dog with the banana-like head was completely attention seeking and could become somewhat of a pain. Sarah found herself being pleasantly surprised.

The customary kiss to welcome in the New Year was quick and to the point. The second was longer and had more meaning, and by the third one Sarah was looking at Ed in a whole new light.

The run-up to Crufts was mental, but Ed supported Sarah all the way. It was like a switch had been flicked and the media had suddenly remembered who Wylie was and what was at stake. Once more, local television and print press hounded Sarah for the opportunity to film and photograph him. It was a circus as everybody fell over themselves trying to get on the Wylie roadshow.

Sarah had assumed it would be a simple case of driving to Birmingham, as Wylie was no longer averse to car journeys. The solution had been to dig out her old dog seatbelt harness: Wylie hated being shut away in the boot space behind the rear passenger seat, but let him ride on the back seat, secured with the seatbelt harness, and he was as happy as Larry. Being chauffeured around like Lord Muck as he stared out of the window at his subjects working and rushing to work was, to Wylie, the most natural thing in the world for a dog to do.

Sarah's plans to head straight to Birmingham, however, went right out the window when an early morning breakfast show called her to ask for a pre-Crufts final appearance. Both Ed and Sarah scratched their heads as they tried to work out how they could travel first to London for a 7 a.m. breakfast show appearance, and then make the long drive north for the midday deadline for the finals of Scruffts at Crufts, which would now include all the winners of the Scruffts six categories, there to decide who was going to be the dog to win the title of the James Wellbeloved Family Crossbreed of the Year 2014.

It became a master planning session between the television production crew and Wylie's support crew but, such was the draw of Wylie's fame, money was no expense for the television production company. A train was booked for the first part of the journey, to London, ensuring Wylie travelled in style to his night in a four-star hotel situated near to the studios. Sarah and Ed accompanied him, carrying the various bags he would need for the course of the next few days. The next morning, a posh car was waiting for them as they emerged into the early morning, pre-rush hour London, and they were whisked off to the studios and Wylie's early morning news slot.

Wylie once more seemed unfazed by the fuss made of him, having his own green room to lounge around in while Ed tried to relax a very nervous Sarah, who had suddenly realised, albeit slightly late, that she was about to be on live national television.

The time came. Rigged up with a hidden microphone, Sarah and Wylie were led along to the set of the studio. There, a pristine sofa and news desk were arranged in the middle of a cluttered studio full of different backdrops and furniture, all ready to be swapped at a moment's notice during commercial breaks.

Sarah and Wylie were ushered in as the previous guests were finishing their interviews.

'And go to VT!' shouted an unseen voice as Sarah was pushed towards the sofa just as a camera man turned round suddenly and ended up punching Sarah squarely in the face.

'Ouch'

Sarah was propelled forward as if nothing had happened to the waiting sofa as if being punched in the face by a camera man was the normal guest experience prior to live television.

The male and female co-presenters sat there grinning fixedly at the cameras, while the now irrelevant former guests were more or less pulled from the couch to make way for Sarah and Wylie.

The male anchor nodded over to Sarah as she tried to desperately focus away from the stinging sensation now spreading rapidly over her face to the fact she was about to be on live national TV and with a quick, 'Hello, this must be Wylie,' smiled back towards the camera, cheesy grin fully loaded.

Sarah braced herself for whatever question was about to be fired her way. She had rattled through in her mind on the drive over every possible question they could ask her . . . and besides now her face hurt. A lot.

The anchorman looked her way: 'So, dog baiting. What is that all about?' he asked, Cheshire-cat grin now replaced by a stern, semi-concerned grin.

Inside, Sarah sighed. 'Dog baiting?' Wylie had been rescued from the depths of despair in Afghanistan, and the anchor wanted to know about dog baiting? He hadn't even introduced Wylie.

As the last guests had run over their allocated time slot, Sarah was given just two minutes and ten seconds of air time. They had travelled all the way to London on the morning of the finals of Crufts, for just two minutes and ten seconds.

'Well, at least I was able to mention Nowzad Dogs once,' she thought to herself, as she too was ushered unceremoniously from the sofa. It was a small consolation prize.

Without any further fanfare, they were ushered immediately outside to the waiting car that would chauffeur them to the National Exhibition Centre in Birmingham, and the event that everything had been leading towards.

It had been a non-stop whirlwind since the second they had parked by the roundabout that led to the long, glass-panelled main entrance to the NEC, the home of Crufts. Escorted through to the arena as if they were dog royalty, Sarah, Ed and the star, Wylie, had been waylaid by the Kennel Club team who had interviewed a jubilant Sarah after Wylie's win at Discover Dogs.

Even the camera crew couldn't hide their excitement and hopes for Sarah and Wylie.

As this was the culmination of countless heats and many months' preparation, the Kennel Club organisers were leaving nothing to chance, and Sarah and Wylie were party to a quick rehearsal before the cameras rolled and the show went live.

Kate Lawler was the judge who would make or break Wylie's bid to be crowned top dog. A former *Big Brother* contestant who has been fairly well-blessed in the looks department, had made her name from her talent for hosting a top listened-to programme on Kerrang! Radio.

Kate herself is a serious dog lover owning two small dogs: Kevin, a teacup Yorkie, and Baxter the Border terrier.

Kate could not refrain from crying a little when Sarah relayed Wylie's story to her during the rehearsal. It was a good sign. In the case of a rescued dog's tale, if you could make the judge cry then you were in with a chance. Or so Sarah hoped, anyway.

Once more under a spotlight, they entered the ring in file: There was Bailey, Most Handsome crossbreed; Sylvy, Prettiest crossbreed; Lola, Child's Best Friend crossbreed; Willow, the eleven-year-old Golden Oldie; Barney, the Good Citizen Scheme crossbreed; and, of course, Wylie, Best Crossbreed Rescue.

It was heart-stopping stuff as Sarah stood in the middle of the ring, shaking badly, whilst Wylie stood perfectly still, calm as could be as the big screens to the side of them displayed the short videos that the Kennel Club had filmed at the home of each finalist, weeks earlier.

Kate walked along the line of finalists, stopping to talk to each one as the videos played. As she reached Wylie, he flopped onto his side, just as he had done for the old lady in the back streets of Kandahar so long ago. Kate stroked and tickled his white-haired tummy as Wylie raised his upper rear leg into the air and relaxed completely.

Kate stood up and leaned over to shout into Sarah's ear to make sure Sarah could hear over the noise of the television screens: 'I can't believe how trusting he is after all he has been through!'

Sarah just nodded in reply as Kate, obviously deep in thought, strolled back to the middle of the arena to make her decision.

Sarah tried desperately to calm herself, sure they wouldn't let her win the competition twice. Had she said enough? She had at least done Wylie's story justice, hadn't she?

But it was too late for any self-doubt. Either way, she had achieved what she had set out to do, by promoting the Nowzad Dogs charity that had helped to rescue Wylie, on the centre stage at Crufts to a live audience.

Kate announced she had made her decision.

Sarah was on tenterhooks; Wylie just standing there looking rather bemused, or maybe even bored, by the whole affair. And, suddenly, as if everything had gone into slow motion, Sarah was picking up on every word that Kate uttered.

'All of these dogs are winners in their own right, I have fallen in love with every single one of them,' Sarah heard her say, before she heard a 'he' when referring to the dog Kate had chosen as the winner. That was all the bitches out of the running, Sarah realised. When Kate said, 'the long journey he has been on', Sarah's pulse quickened as it sunk in that it could be Wylie she was talking about.

Kate finished by saying how he had let her tickle his tummy.

'Oh my God!' Sarah's head was spinning as Kate looked over towards Wylie and simply shouted into the microphone: 'WYLIE!'

Wylie was the winner of Scruffts James Wellbeloved Family Crossbreed Dog 2014.

It was unbelievable. Feelings of shock and pride rushed through Sarah as she knelt down to hug her canine hero. She was so proud of him, even if he didn't actually have any idea what was happening.

As Sarah knelt down, Wylie flipped his front paws onto her shoulders and, for a moment, they both were on the same level. 'Well done, Afghan,' Sarah said to him, as Wylie acknowledged her with a fluffy tail wave. He was truly a superstar rescue dog.

Sarah, too, had every right to be chuffed with herself – she had beaten the odds and won the event for the second time.

The camera crew rushed in for an interview as, off to one side of the arena, along the Scruffts Hall of Fame wall, Wylie's gilt-framed photograph was already being lofted up high and fixed in its rightful place as the champion of crossbreed dogs.

Sarah was almost too overwhelmed to speak as the cameras lined her up for the interview and the quote they were desperately seeking: 'I am so incredibly proud of him. The journey he has been on from his beginnings in Afghanistan, where he was near death so many times, to now be in the main ring at Crufts, is just amazing. By winning he represents all the rescue dogs in all the world. He has changed my life and is the most wonderful companion you could possibly wish for.'

Wylie just wagged his quarter-length tail. He was bored. It was time to go and find Ben and yank on his tail some more.

Afterword

Wylie lay down on the cool, tiled floor. He wagged his tail once at a fellow member of his pack: Milo flopped over beside him and more or less fell instantly asleep. Ben was already curled up – his tail firmly hidden from view – in the well-worn and hairy dog bed across the floor, still tired from a long walk around the farm earlier.

For Wylie, food was so easy to come by these days. No more hunting and poking through smelly rubbish or being afraid of other dogs attacking him. Now it was brought to him twice a day. He had almost forgotten what it felt like to be really hungry, often for days at a time.

That feeling was so long ago.

The little old lady that had fed him by the rusting car had been forgotten too, in the passing of time. And the Australian woman who had gently cared for him time and time again when he had hobbled home, battered and bleeding, was now just a shadowy face that he could no longer fully picture. Now he had adopted this slightly mad woman called Sarah who never stopped talking, and who doted on him.

At first, he had been constantly worried that she was going to leave him, and it had stopped him trying to get too friendly with her – he was sad when he kept losing his friends. But then he had relaxed into the routine that she had for him: she fed him, went out for a time and then came home, made a fuss of him, walked him and fed him some more. She was always there for him. Although he still wasn't quite sure what he was called. For a long while he had been Wylie but now it was sometimes 'Herbert', then 'Afghan'. He was confused. But he knew her tone of voice and whenever she said one of those names it indicated she either had something tasty for him or, as was often more, it was when he was sitting on the table and she meant for him to get off.

And then there were always visitors to the cottage who wanted to make a fuss of him, and he got especially excited when he saw Bruce and Grandma Rose, both people he wished he could see more of. They always made a fuss of him. They were good people to him. And there was Ed who fed him loads when Sarah wasn't looking. He liked Ed.

Life was good. He was forgetting the pain and torment of his former life back in the desolate place that to him, now, was just a bad dream. He had mixed feelings about the dog shows. They had been fun at first, but he was slowly getting bored with the travel and all the standing around. But he had clearly done something right, as Sarah had been so happy with him. And he had a feeling that he wouldn't be doing any more shows anyway because, during the last one, as the crowd had hushed, waiting for the results during the finals, Sarah had leant down to him and promised that if he won the event, there would be no more dog shows. So he had done what he always did and not given up on people.

The cropped-eared puppy scavenged slowly along the rubbish-strewn banks of the side road that led to the bombed-out palace that still stood, proudly and majestic, at the end of the grand Darulaman road in Kabul.

The pup was hungry. And cold. It was a chilling wind. Now and again it would stumble as it misjudged its footing on the rocky, windswept desert ground.

The noise of a van screeching suddenly to a stop nearby scared it; the sounds of approaching footsteps forced it to scurry for the safety of the rocky shelter that it called home.

A hand grabbed roughly for the unexpectedly fast-moving pup but mistimed the action and the pup broke free to dart under the safety of the largish rock that gave it shelter.

Which turned out be a good thing.

Under the rock, already sheltering, was the little pup's sister, scared and hungry too.

The light from the mid-morning sun was blocked out as a face appeared in the opening to the cramped den.

'Hello there, you two. It's going to be all right.' The voice was nothing like the pup had heard before. There was no harsh tones. It sounded soothing. The docked-eared pup had experienced people before – when a hand had reached in, and painfully taken its ears.

But the owner of this face was smiling.

'Dr Hadi!' The voice boomed back towards the van to be heard over the noise of the traffic. 'Please get the gloves. We have two more candidates for the shelter!'

I stood up and looked down at the concealed hiding place that the two pups were holed up in. The pup had been lucky. If I had grabbed the wandering pup on my first attempt, then I would have missed her sister.

I had rushed from the van without bothering to put on my jacket when ordering Wahidullah to stop the vehicle when I had first seen the pup disappear behind some rubbish. The road was just too busy for an abandoned pup to be roaming along. But I didn't feel the cold as I waited for Dr Hadi to arrive – I was far too absorbed in figuring out how to get the two little guys out of the hole without being bitten.

With Dr Hadi lying next to me in the dirt and discarded rubbish along the side of the road, together we scooped out the two pups. We had made a difference to two more lives. Darla (after the palace) and Jangly (Dari for 'rubbish') as they were later named, were rescued that day from a very short and unforgiving life on the streets of Kabul. From the Nowzad Dogs animal shelter in Kabul, both dogs went on to be rehomed together in England.

Wylie, ultimately, was one of the lucky ones of many that share his pitiful story in the harsh reality of modern-day Afghanistan. And surviving to tell his 'tail' paves the way for ever more Wylies to be rescued.

The Work of Nowzad

Nowzad Dogs is working tirelessly to make a difference in Afghanistan and has progressed so much since the events of this book took place. We now have moved into a clinic and cattery of our own and our dog shelter is purpose built and can accommodate over 100 dogs.

We have started small but with your help we can achieve more. We are working towards a humane trap neuter release programme to reduce the epidemic stray dog population problem which, in turn, will reduce the incidence of canine rabies.

Every little we do makes a difference, because we are not just walking away – and we hope you won't too. If you enjoyed this book, please recommend it to friends, family and other dog lovers. It is our advert to tell the 'tail' of the non-profit organisation and dogs like Wylie, who desperately need our support in Afghanistan. If you can advertise us on your website or have another idea to raise our profile, please do get in touch.

Donations are always needed so the charity can continue to make a difference in Afghanistan, either via our office:

Nowzad Dogs, PO Box 39, Plymouth, PL2 9AU,

or via our website www.nowzad.com

Our American supporters can make a tax deductible donation to the Nowzad Dogs charity via www.nowzad.org

Mission Statement: To relieve the suffering of animals, predominantly stray and abandoned dogs, in need of care and attention, and to provide and maintain rescue facilities for the care and treatment of such animals, especially the dogs of Afghanistan.

Registered charity (non-profit) in the UK, number 1119185 and a Not For Profit 501(c3) in the USA.

Nowzad Dogs – making a difference one dog at a time . . .

An invitation from the publisher

Join us at www.hodder.co.uk, or follow us
on Twitter @hodderbooks to be a part of
our community of people who love the very
best in books and reading.

Whether you want to discover more about a book
or an author, watch trailers and interviews, have the
chance to win early limited editions, or simply browse
our expert readers' selection of the very best books,
we think you'll find what you're looking for.

And if you don't, that's the place to tell us what's missing.

We love what we do, and we'd love you to be a part of it.

www.hodder.co.uk

@hodderbooks

HodderBooks

HodderBooks